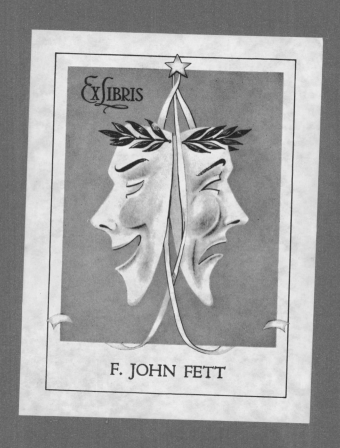

Costume on the Stage

Artia

Costume on the Stage

A Book of Costume Designs

Edited by *František Tröster*
with Introduction by *Ludmila Vachtová*
and Text by *Milan Lukeš*

Graphic design by
Stanislav Kolíbal and Václav Boštík
Translated by Ota Vojtíšek
Designed and produced by
ARTIA • Prague
© 1962 by ARTIA

Printed in Czechoslovakia
S 1110

List of Plays

INTRODUCTION

The problems of theatrical expression during its thousand year development have linked and mingled its individual components in a complex organism to such an extent that it would not be wise to prefer one to the detriment of another. Our pleasures as well as requirements have become more refined — our idea of the theatre is represented today not only by the actor and the play or the theme improvised — there is the producer, the extensive stage equipment and all those who know how to handle it, the stage designer and the costume designer. The reason for naming these two last is not that we intend to deprive them of the lime-light; on the contrary, the share of the plastic art component of theatrical expression is getting into the foreground and often helps to shape the producer's idea as well as the actor's action.

Clothes make the man but man makes the clothes. The theatrical costume designer makes a little of both at the same time — man as well as clothes. The theatrical costume designer is neither tailor nor fashionable *arbiter elegantiae*. He does not create dresses for society, beach or sport but defines the ideas of his Ophelias, Cyranos, Chimènes and Don Juans. Fashion — or rather a general prevalence of taste in a given historical period — naturally affects theatrical costume; on the other hand, although this might seem at first glance paradoxical, theatrical costume affects fashion. As far as I know, it occurred only once in the history of the modern theatre that Christian Dior, the Fashion King, was asked to create the showy ballet costumes for the *Thirteen Dances* by Rolland le Petit for the performance at the Ballet des Champs-Elysées theatre (1947), while under the influence of the performance of Diaghilev's Russian Ballet the one desire of ladies of fashion was that their gowns were at least a little à la Bakst or à la Benois. Fashion was similarly affected by the theatrical costumes of Christian Bérard or, so that we do not look for examples only in the life of past generations, let us recall the revolution in the headdresses, materials and fashion lines, caused in Paris by the performance of the Peking opera.

Theatrical costume designing is an independent branch which has little in common with the general method of fashion designing. Its independence applies to the working up of the cut and material as well as the whole conception. As regards material, the phantasy of the costume designer is practically unrestricted; it is left to his discretion by which combinations he will achieve the final shape of the figures, whether he will contrast leather with lace, synthetic fibres with natural ones or the nobility of velvet with sack-cloth. In love and art everything is permitted: an aluminium foil and a fish-

1

ing net may achieve an equally noble effect as a "snowdrift" of genuine Flanders lace on Spanish brocade. The artist has a choice of two possibilities: he can either respect the material (as in the Renaissance), emphasise by suitable use its texture till he achieves the illusion of an optical impression, or he may neglect it (as in the Baroque), or even violate it to such an extent that the cloth ceases to exist as such, becoming a mere plastic material for spinning, modelled by a creative artist's imagination and intention, a spinning material which under new conditions and in new relations is able to give a new testimony of its changed existence, being able to substitute, deceive and express.

In the case of pictures and statues we usually overestimate the technical aspect of their creation. We are liable to introduce this approach also into the judging of theatrical costume — we admire a "correctly" sewn-on button as much as daringly laid-on paste or a tasteful wash of ultramarine. Theatrical costume, however, is no mere tailoring. The design, submitted for realization, does not represent an analysis of cut but rather brings forth the person who will realize it into the atmosphere of stage character: it comments on its appearance and presumed behaviour, it draws attention to the maximum extent of movement or measure of immobility used and exploited by this character in the actor's action, it determines the colour and scale and contours, giving an overall impression rather than accurate instructions for execution. It goes without saying that a great deal depends on the tailor's intelligence as to how he will understand the design and what consequences he will draw from it for himself.

If he, who transforms the idea of the costume designer into three-dimensional shape were only a tailor of good clothes, he would naturally attempt to soften all the extravagant features of the costume to give it the becoming aspect of a lounge suit. Workers in theatrical tailors' shops, however, must understand that what in the eyes of a good couturier would seem an awful eccentricity: namely, that perfect hem-stitching is less important than perfect maintaining of the artistic idea, that the deformations of individual parts of the costume are not the result of the draughtsman's whim but that they are functional deformations, functional in the sense of the stage character, formed by the costume and its actor. It is not enough to say that the costume is well tailored. The question is whether it is made correctly, whether the tailor's craft did not weaken the artist's intention. The road from the design to its realization is purposive, though seldom smooth. Its result depends on cooperation of the costume designer with the tailor's shop, and on supplementing and correcting of the designer's idea and the finished product in the material.

Theatrical costume, therefore, is never a common fashion dress, even if plays in contemporary settings by Steinbeck, Beckett, Ionesco, Miller or Osborne are played. Theatrical costume, however, is never a precise historical costume, even if it is Caesar, Hans Sachs or Cid who are revived on the scene. Its task is not the task of a documentary film or the reconstruction of an historical event. Even if the text of the play emphatically orders that its action takes place in April, 1621, the happenings of this date have been long forgotten and we shall never be able to reconstruct them emotionally from the viewpoint of those who experienced it.

Should we wish to adhere pedantically to historical authenticity, we could never appreciate Blake's interpretation of the *Divine Comedy* or Doré's illustration to *Don Quixote* or Picasso's creations based on Ovid's *Metamorphoses*. Although our visits to museums of period fashions, where, in their showcases, inexpressible fragrances of former dignities, loves and adulteries decay in the remnants of textiles, may be exciting and full of nostalgy, they will always be only museum pieces, only sources for our fantasy.

Historical costume is for the costume designer the same kind of material as the text of the role. It is his task to interpret it by all his imaginative power. He is entitled to lift it into another sphere in which it would shine as a gem which never ages, by the new and unexpected intensity of its cut. He must use the historical costume as a documentary material which gives him incentives, stimulating him to individual expression as to individual attitude. Contemporary theatre design has nothing in common with "thinking in a corset" which to such an extent "laced up" the nineteenth century and the traces of which faithfully accompany all notes on theatrical costume of that time. Carefully observing the number of fancy trimmings necessary for a grenadier's jacket and prescribing a taffeta skirt or serge trousers, they considered themselves to be realists. They were, however, mere imitators. They wished to have on the stage things looking as life-like as possible but they stifled them with details. The result of such activities may be an interesting exhibit for the Musée Grévin, but it could be never called theatrical costume in the present sense of its meaning.

Fashion, however, is not born in a vacuum. It very subtly reflects social conditions. A theatrical play, set or originating in a certain historical period, must somehow deal with these conditions. Even where it does not analyze them, it gives a certain testimony of them. The designer shaping the characters of such a play must consider all these facts. In addition he must add his own testimony. It depends on the talent of the costume designer how he will adapt the play to historical milieu. If he understands this milieu, i. e., if he realizes not only the shape of the head-dress in the late Gothic period but also the thoughts which passed through Gothic heads, he cannot be reconciled to a mere fashionable cliché or satisfied with the expert knowledge of the antique collector. The creative artist's imagination may be stimulated by the general shape or colour of historical dress, or from the balanced harmony of splendour and proportion suddenly emerges an eloquent detail, the use of which may signify a great deal for the general composition of contemporary costume: exaggerated use of jewellery in the Renaissance will suddenly draw attention to certain effeminate features in men's clothes, ribbons and faveurs will authenticate the image of the dandy from the period of the Thirty Years War, etc.

As the designing of the theatrical costume belongs to the realm of arts, it is left at the discretion of its creator which source of inspiration he will neglect and which he will prefer and further develop. It is impossible to say several things simultaneously —the words would suffocate us. Conciseness of expression is the best testimony to the strength of an idea.

The actor's action takes place in the area of the stage. The actor's costume is intended for the same locality. A large stage focuses our attention on the contours of the costume and gestures, on coloured shapes, and on the overall appearance of the material used. It makes possible a striking use of light which can unify all costumes or add a final touch elevating the actor's figure to a monument or dissolving it into an atmospheric sfumato. The intrinsic quality of material is here less important than its effectiveness in large rhythmical surfaces — nervous folds of light fabrics may be contrasted with the majestic flowing of velvet draperies, etc. On a large stage the overall appearance of the costume will be most important. A small stage, on the contrary, requires emphasis on detail: the colour of nail varnish, the type of the wig, a shoe clasp, a glove or a jewel will be nearer to the atmosphere of the role than a wild grimace of a made-up face. Here come to the fore also the intimate qualities of materials — fur lining or embroidery then cease to be only an ornament, an extra luxury or an expression of the theatre's financial status — but they actually enter into the play. The details do not tire the audience by an exhausting enumeration but permit them to associate and combine ideas. Work with detail, however, should be used only sparingly: if we use a great number of details, we shall not be able to see the wood for the trees.

Although the designing of theatrical costume is an individual problem its author must take into account its twofold dependence: its relation to the architectural design of the *décor* (a dependence only seemingly external) and its relation to other roles. Best results are achieved when the *décor* and costumes are designed by one artist. In order to achieve maximum effect, the *décor* and costume should be of uniform design. An impressive *décor* sometimes collapses as a house of cards when the actors appear on the scene. The scale of the costume suddenly does not correspond with the scale of the architectonic layout. In these cases, it is sometimes the stage designer who is accused of looking neither right nor left. Another time the blame falls on the costume designer. Frequently it is the producer who is guilty, because he did not succeed in synchronizing both conceptions in good time. Cooperation of the two designers should be the starting point and the goal.

When designing costumes the artist must set out from the whole list of characters. If he elaborates in details character after character, then he lets himself be transported too much by their individual atmosphere. If he treats it as if it were unique, he cannot express the mutual relation of the characters of the play. Still, it is just this inter-relation of characters, their sympathies and contradictions, which affect the spectator. The composition of costumes should, therefore, maintain tension or concentration according to the character of the play, by means of an arabesque shape and colour.

This arabesque may successfully imbue with rhythm the architectural plans of the *décor*. In a scene full of extras the dress designer can even organize them into compositional units, between which he will intensify and diminish the tension of the play.

Although the costume for a certain stage-character, when considered in isolation, may be extremely effective, its true value will show in confrontation with costumes of other roles. The costumes of one play should all be members of one family, maintaining their colour scale as well as shape cadence. Only then can they fully assert themselves as a solo part with the accompaniment of a suitable combination of major, minor and even dissonant chords.

Contemporary theatrical costume strikingly denaturalizes itself: it does not insist on archeologically precise details but searches for meanings and "subtexts". Denaturalization of the costume does not imply depersonification of the role, on the contrary: a well-designed costume helps the actor to shape his gestures, it forces him to adhere to a certain kind of behaviour ("clothes make the man"), thus helping him to complete the character of the role.

Simultaneously with the changes of opinion regarding the function of theatrical costume, its present form goes hand in hand with definite principles of a certain theatre production. For example, Brecht's Berliner Ensemble emphasizes especially the material aspect of costumes, MCHAT adheres to the "veristic" style, even to the most accurate and detailed historical reconstruction, Jean Villar has elevated costume to an absolutely dominating element on an empty stage. Bauhaus's experimental scene which neglected all historical aspects and designed costumes only according to their immediate aesthetic values, was an extreme solution of the problems of theatrical costume. True, when designing theatrical costume one is not bound by any restrictions, nevertheless its designer, especially when working on plays with historical themes, must respect some aspects on which he is dependent. First of all, he expresses the present attitude to the historical material, which though strange to us, appears on the scene and therefore has a right to independent existence and enters into a certain relation with our ideas. The actor expresses this relation by his conception of the role, the designer by his conception of the costume. Further, the designer expresses his attitude to the dramatist of the past. This attitude, too, is affected by the time: where past generations were able to enjoy buffoonery we suddenly perceive a definite trend of social criticism, where a pompous pathos used to storm, we try to introduce a matter-of-fact *milieu*, where poetic simile was used, we prefer fact. We adapt our dramatic heritage to the present time, present perception, present imagination. This adaptability of interpretations is the *raison d'être* of the theatre. It gives it the possibility of development and guarantees its vitality. Like the producer and the actor, the costume designer, too, must find a bridge between these different time levels. The words have changed. The subject has remained. Thorwaldsen's antiquity is not Picasso's antiquity, thousands of years in the development of society will make the *première* of Sophocles' *Oedipus* different from its performance today. In the designing of costume there are no obstacles of dogma: the costume for the same role, designed again and again throughout the centuries, will have always new solutions, conditioned by the state of society, its loves and hatreds.

Even when we admit the individual characteristics of the designer's taste, his invention, his skill in draughtsmanship, the result is always the visual representation of the dramatic text.

The costume designs in our publication document a certain attitude to the designer's task according to the principles indicated. The very selection of plays is complicated: their subject does not always cover the period of their origin: Verdi selects his motif from ancient Egypt, Wagner turns to medieval themes, Shakespeare exploits ancient history. Although the task is intricate, it must be solved lucidly. The costume designer must give unto Caesar what is Caesar's and unto Shakespeare what is Skakespeare's. He must balance several aspects: the character of the play, the author's personality, and the spectator of the twentieth century.

Costume designs in our book respect these conditions and in addition maintain a personal style as well as a different conception of expression, which varies according to the character and maturity of individual creative artists. The choice of designers naturally does not show the whole range of costume creation, as we can see it on Czechoslovak stages. On the other hand, it is not a haphazard selection — the designers have had common ideas from the very beginnings of their career and they are all graduates of the Stage Designing branch of the Prague Academy of Arts. Thanks to the creative and pedagogical activities of Professor František Tröster, this school, during the sixteen years of its existence, has trained many artists, capable of fulfilling all the requirements on contemporary stage *décor*.

The extensive experience of František Tröster who has influenced the development of Czechoslovak stage designing for the past thirty years and whose work has several times received international recognition, makes itself felt in the designing of *décor* and costume. František Tröster, an accomplished architect, masters the space of the stage and emphasizes its division by his costume designs. The demand for a uniform *décor* and costume is for him a matter of course — as he has proved in hundreds of his stage *décors*, in which he always knew how to place the costume. His conception of costumes is exclusively sculptural — he always gives correct dimensions to the stage-character's body, the deformations of which, in so far as he uses them, have always a definite meaning for the role. Tröster concentrates on the whole, he does not only cut the clothes but always models the characters. To achieve his scenic intention he studies

Daumier as well as medieval woodcuts. Tröster loves experimenting and he is not afraid to overstate.

The starting point of Branč's costume designs is the richness of colour, derived from the historical atmosphere and adjusted for the dramatic tension of the respective play. He does not emphasize shape — individual figures, clothed in a continuous cover of colour material are differentiated by ornamental details. The aesthetic aim of Branč's costumes is in the symbolic evaluation of colour and its significance for the spectator.

Dimitri Kadrnožka, a skillful draftsman, prefers the linear arabesque which endows his designs with a touch of caricature. He submits with delight the heroes of Aristophanes' *Lysistrata* as well as the braggart of Plautus to this criticism and though his drawings have a trend to burlesque epic poetry, he can, however, discipline himself into a fully serious expression.

The main advantage of costumes by J. Kadrnožková is a careful consideration of material. She experiments with materials, combines them, the striving for a definite expression of the material is obvious already in her designs which generally take the form of *collage*. Her designs are sober — the definiteness and objectivity of the shape and the figure's contours are more important for her than the look of the drawing. Kadrnožková accurately follows the text of the play, and combining intellect with intuition, finds its present meaning.

Stanislav Kolíbal has intentionally deprived theatrical costume of all epithets and says only the essential. This final expression is preceded by a number of long imaginary conversations of the designing artist with the playwright and the *dramatis persona*. Kolíbal's costumes correspond to his idea of the actor and dramatic character — expression of this is sometimes summed up by a practical detail, such as a string of pearls, a hat or a scarf.

The precise line of Jan Skalický's designs, showing in places even a Baroque-like calligraphic rhythm, knows not only how to accurately register his idea of the stage character but also to express the designer's emotional relationship to it. In spite of the multitude of ideas and their innumerable variations he always bears in mind technical possibilities of costume execution. He knows the requirements of materials and their combinations and is well acquainted with the work of the tailor. Skalický makes the most of the costume details — he knows how to elevate them to a more important position and form.

The costume designs by Oldřich Smutný illustrate the atmosphere of the play — his buoyant, almost nervous rendering neglects details, leaving them at the discretion of further technical processing, but accurately expresses the colour atmosphere of all the characters considered to be real individualities. In the case of individual costumes he does not divide attention between their overall impression and individual details — he is concerned with a summary conception, with a coordination of all characters which should manifest itself on the stage by unity of colour.

Vladimír Tesař has concentrated on the contours of the shape, on the linear aspect of his designs. He knows how to characterize his shapes precisely and concisely. He is sober in colour — this does not mean, of course, that he is poor in colour — the method by which he achieved such fine results in his work as costume designer. If we compare his designs for the *Representatio Mariarium* with the colouring of late Gothic panels, we see the remarkable talent with which he is able to display a single consistent coloured accord and to develop variations on its theme.

The designs in this book can be described as an endeavour to create contemporary historical theatrical costume. Eight different attitudes of eight different stage designers prove that in this work there exists a number of possibilities, that the certain conventions necessary for this art are by far not so restricted and stagnant as it would appear at first glance. By respecting the importance and range of individual dramas and their authors, the designer can also present them to the modern spectator and in contemporary language of visual arts. Thus they help to foster the visual component of the performance which has the same importance as the text of the play and the accomplishments of the actors.

The Plays and the Designs

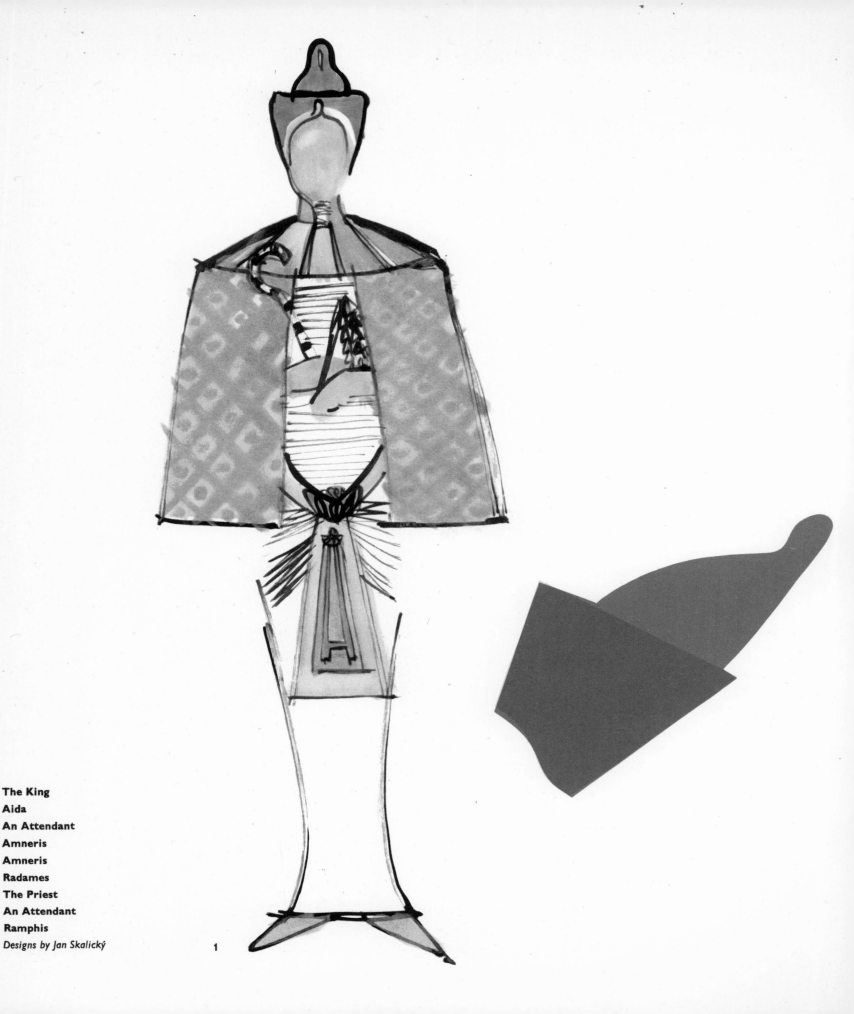

Designs by Jan Skalický

1

GIUSEPPE VERDI

Aida

There are works which originate slowly and with difficulty, and there are others which are the fruit of several weeks or months of happy creative effort. Some works are created from immense internal impulse, an irrepressible and irresistible incitement, while other works are occasional, originating from outside impulses. The former, it seems, are entitled to immortality — the latter are said to be ephemeral and will only be remembered by connoisseurs.

It is not always so. Are not four months an incredibly short time for the creation of so complicated and elaborate a work as an opera? It is hardly possible to recollect a more striking example of a genuinely external impulse than a Government order requiring the opera to be ready for the official inauguration of the Suez Canal? All the same the fifty-five year old composer Verdi, who before and afterwards took much more time to compose his operas, wrote under these circumstances an immortal work, which is perhaps the most frequently played and popular of them all.

During those four months the composer's mind was wholly concentrated on that unusually bizarre material which the librettist Antonio Ghislanzoni had elaborated for him after Mariett's story. Verdi stimulated his fantasy by a study of archaeological monuments, paintings without perspective from ancient Egypt, severe, monumental and sombre religious architecture and especially by the scant knowledge of music and musical instruments of that period. He cooperated closely with Ghislanzoni, adapting his libretto to his musical ideas.

In December 1871, as had been firmly fixed in advance, the introductory strokes of *Aida* were heard for the first time in Cairo. The great day of triumph of human ingenuity and technique was also a great day of human fantasy and art.

In Verdi's winning music there was magnificently developed the tragic love story where love is crushed at the tense moment when it encounters the interests of the State, of the country. In vain did the leader of the Egyptian armies, the brave hero Radames, fight for the right to love Aida, the daughter

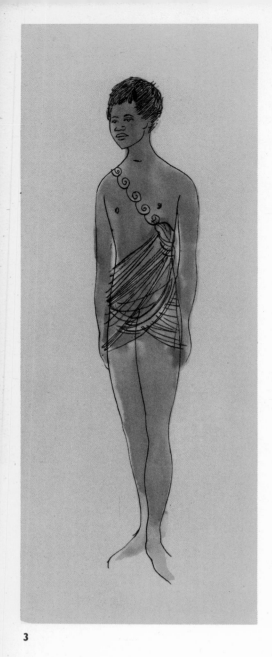

of the Ethiopean King, who is living in his country — unrecognised — as a slave. Impassioned love leads to unintentional treason, Radames is tried and must undergo a terrible punishment — to be buried alive in an underground cave. It is not his fate, however, to die alone: when the priests close the exit to the cave with a heavy boulder Radames finds that the loving Aida is sharing the terrifying dark cell with him. The lovers who were unable to love each other while alive could not be prevented from dying in each other's arms.

3

4

4

6

6

7

8

9

7

SOPHOKLES   *Oedipus*

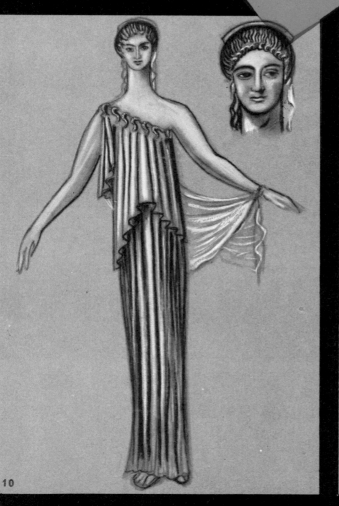

10

11

12

Of Sophocles, the cleverest of the great triad of tragic poets of ancient Greece, the comediograph Frynichos wrote: "Blessed was Sophocles, happy in his long life, fate as well as talent, happy to have written so many beautiful tragedies and well ending a life which had not known misfortune."

As a matter of fact very few men of genius in art can compete with him in regard to the respect, even reverence, which he already received during his life which lasted nearly ninety years. Sophocles lived a full rich life and the list of his great works is rich, too: they number about a hundred, although only a fraction of them has been handed down to us — a mere seven. Even this negligible part is, however, enough to entitle Sophocles even today to be ranked with the greatest of the great — and if only one play were preserved — namely *Oedipus* — his title to greatness would be the same.

13

The importance of *Oedipus* is truly that of a founder. Sophocles was the first who created the psychological figure of a tragic hero, the first who truthfully depicted the superhuman fight of man against fate, the first who discovered the secret of extreme dramatic simplicity, austerity and concentration. Anyone who later on studied and selected the most effective plots of world dramatic literature, did not omit *Oedipus*, and in the art of evoking dramatic tension Sophocles has remained unsurpassed.

The simplicity of the plot betrays a genius. Oedipus, having solved the secret of the Sphinx, leads Thebes to prosperity — nevertheless a curse is cast on the city. The new ruler does his best to discover its cause

15

14

16

17

and to find the culprit. It appears that he himself is the culprit — being the involuntary murderer of his father, the former King, and having, in addition, married the widowed Queen and had children by her. When the truth is revealed Oedipus chooses his punishment himself: he puts out his eyes.

The happy Sophocles was the first to give content to that which centuries after him was called the tragic feeling of life.

18

19

20

ARISTOPHANES

Lysistrata

For many a dramatist, novelist and even screen-writer the *Lysistrata* of Aristophanes has been a source of inspiration. The history of art registers a series of attempts to enhance and transfer into another historic situation or artistic genre the eternally fresh — and as is seen in its own way — the inimitable comic art of the Greek dramatist. After the more than two thousand years which have elapsed since its *première*, *Lysistrata* does not belong to those works which are admired and quoted by everybody, but hardly known by anyone: its popularity also among the broad masses of the lay public almost fully corresponds to its importace as the first great comedy of European dramatic art.

Its comic intrigue dazzles by its very simplicity. When the so-called Peloponnesian war between Athens and Sparta lasted insupportably long — and it lasted really the full ten years — Lysistrata, a beautiful and clever Athenian, discovered a method how to bring it to an end. Her idea was soon realised: she called her companions, afflicted by the war as herself, and submitted a daring proposal to them — to come to an agreement and bind themselves by solemn oath that all the Athenian wives and sweethearts would refuse their men that which they had formerly gladly and willingly granted: namely until such a time when the men would conclude a peace. This surprising proposition was at the beginning accepted with a certain hesitation; when, however, the envoy of the enemy Spartan camp had also accepted it on behalf of her companions, the men's destiny on both sides was decided.

21

22

Aristophanes, of course, was still able to achieve a multitude of irresistible comic situations. The men, whom this women's conspiracy surprised just at the moment when they were enjoying the fight to the full, began to boast, then grew excited, begged, threatened and raged. The women, however, were adamant in their resolution, although they did not like this voluntary renunciation; even though attempts to desert occurred in her ranks, the energetic Lysistrata succeeded in bringing back at the last moment all the would-be

23

25

24

women deserters and in renewing order. Thus the men were quickly forced to make peace and shake hands with their former enemies — in order to be able to return to the arms of their wives and sweethearts.

Love, asserts Aristophanes in this excellent comedy, must, after all, be stronger then any fighting instincts. Love has, therefore, the last word in Aristophanes' play which ends in a joyful apotheosis of amorous feeling and life in peace.

27

26

19 First Old Man
20 Lysistrata
21 A Citizen of Athens
22 An Athenian Woman
23 Second Old Man
24 A Citizen of Athens
25 Myrrhine
26 Lampito
27 Slave

Designs by Dimitri Kadrnožka

17

WILLIAM SHAKESPEARE

Julius Caesar

When Shakespeare began to work some time in 1599 on his "Roman Tragedy" he already had to his credit most of his historical plays, a series of excellent comedies and two tragedies. In addition he had selected the theme from ancient history; the man who knew "little Latin and less Greek" was bold enough to enter the domain of learned dramatists, graduates of one or both universities.

In Elizabethan drama there exists a whole number of tragedies on the great figures of antiquity. As a rule they excel in elaborate dramatic structure, exquisite dialogue and especially historic truthfulness and careful detail. Their authors worked at them for quite a long time and before they began to write they had thoroughly studied historical material in order to avoid anachronism and other mistakes. Those works really correspond to knowledge of ancient history of that time — which was not little; anyone who studies them today, learns a great deal about the period dealt with by these works.

Those, however, who return to these works today, are regrettably few: these works are, as a matter of fact, in the best event creations of cold marble beauty, in which the unique fantasy of the artist is overshadowed by scientific love of facts.

As regards historical accuracy, of course, Shakespeare's *Julius Caesar* cannot compete with these "marble tragedies". Similarly, from the point of view, of construction, this tragedy could not satisfy at that time: the hero, whose name the drama bears, dies in the middle of the play — and is in actual fact no hero of drama at all. Only a short section of Ceasar's life is depicted here, only his last few days: the famous Ides of March of the year 44 are approaching, Caesar arriving at the Capitol to take part in the session of the Senate is stabbed below the statue of Pompey by the daggers of Optimate conspirators.

Although Caesar's name is in the title of the play, Shakespeare was not interested in him and his destiny to such an extent as to make him the central figure of his tragedy. He did not devote himself to him as he did to Hamlet — who was probably nearest to his heart — or to Othello or Lear, and was not interested in him even in the way as with Iago or Macbeth.

The real hero of this tragedy is Brutus, who is here also what we call a genuine Shakespearean figure. This image of Hamlet, and possibly also a certain preparation for it, is one of the most beautiful dramatic characters which Shakespeare ever created, and his tragedy is not only Shakespeare's masterpiece but one of the greatest plays of all time.

Designs by Dimitri Kadrnožka

28   29

30

31

21

32

33

34

35

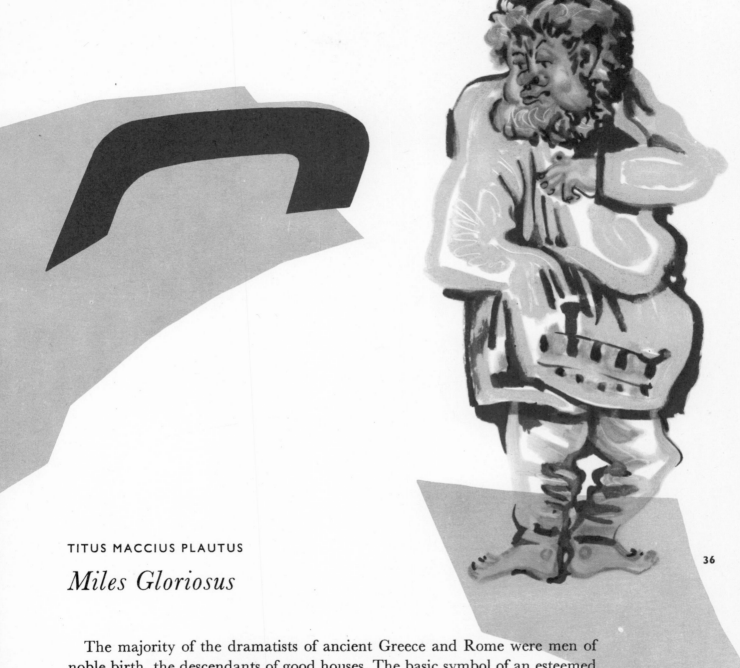

36

TITUS MACCIUS PLAUTUS

Miles Gloriosus

The majority of the dramatists of ancient Greece and Rome were men of noble birth, the descendants of good houses. The basic symbol of an esteemed citizen in Rome were three names which he could use. The author of *The Boastful Soldier* had at first one name only — and his origin was extremely plebeian, even suspect.

In the first place our author was no Roman by birth: he was born about 254 B. C. at Sarsina and led a life appropriate to his low birth. He was a soldier at the time of constant conquests and the great fight of Rome with its strongest competing power: Carthage. He was an actor who performed in rude local burlesque shows, and since the members of "his" troupe were also slaves or at least liberated slaves there is good reason to suppose that Titus — as he was called at the time — was originally also a slave. Then he attempted to make his living as a merchant but failed. He found another means of livelihood — he used to wander from house to house with a hand-mill, grinding the grain for customers while they waited. At that time — he was already forty-five years of age — it occurred to him that he could improve his lot and exploit his experience from his actor's past: he wrote his first two comedies while still a wayfaring miller.

What kind of roles Titus played one is well able to imagine from his appearance. It was not exactly representative but rather unprepossessing, even rousing laughter: he was, as a matter of fact, a red-haired obese man who had to wear strikingly big shoes — so they started to call him Plautus, i. e. Flatfoot. He had an ingrained sense of humour — and spared no one, not even himself. This is testified to by the numerous allusions in his comedies as well as by the fact that when his fame irresistibly spread and he became the most popular author of his time, to whom Rome granted citizenship, thus permitting him to use three names, as a Roman-born subject, he composed those names as follows: Titus Maccius (derived from Maccus, "clown" — and this epithet he selected himself) — Plautus.

It is said that Plautus wrote about one hundred and thirty comedies — of

38

39

40

41

28

which only twenty-one have survived. Our playwright, however, did not bother much about these plots; he simply used those which he had learnt to know from the Greek dramatist Menander. Those conventional intrigues on prodigal sons, stingy fathers and their naughty sweethearts he freely combined — or occasionally only combined two in succession (as in the case of *The Boastful Soldier*) but he succeeded in imbuing them with the contemporary language which was spoken in military camps and in the markets — and what is more important — with contemporary types.

Especially his types of clever servant-slaves (the most famous of them being Pseudolus) who served as a model to numerous modern European dramatists, with Shakespeare and Molière at the head, excel in that gallery of Plautian figures. And last but not least, Plautus created that excellent type of mendacious officer who boasts of exceptional successes in war as well as in bed and who since that time has not disappeared from world literature. His Pyrgopolinices or Miles Gloriosus is throughout a direct, though distant, precursor of the renowned Sir John Falstaff of Shakespeare.

35 Milfidipa, a Slave
36 Palaestrio
37 Pyrgopolinices
38 Aktrotelencium – a Piper
39 Filokomasium
40 Artotrogus, the Parasite
41 Periplektomenus, an Old Man
42 Kario, the Cook
Designs by Dimitri Kadrnožka

29

42

Representatio Mariarum

With the decline and destruction of the ancient world even its drama perished. For the best part of five or six centuries drama in Europe was practically non-existent; a feeble flame flickered only in the performances of itinerant players and jesters.

The Roman Catholic Church, as the controlling power in the Middle Ages, did not admit the revival of the pagan drama of antiquity. This tradition was interrupted only by the advent of the Renaissance which turned *ad fontes*, first to the Roman theatre and then to the lifegiving source of Aeschylus, Sophocles, Euripides and Aristophanes. Let us not, however, anticipate and let us rather return from that famous revival to the pre-millenial era. At that time drama made a new start without taking into account the preceding values.

By the ninth century, during the Easter celebrations, there appeared its very beginning; a chanted dialogue or *tropus* recited by a choir divided into two parts or antiphonal groups. Soon afterwards there appeared the first characters whose small parts were still accompanied by chorus. An angel "acted" here, guarding the tomb of Christ, and the three Marys. These three women came to the sepulchre to anoint Christ's body. The angel asked them: "*Quem quaeritis in sepulchro . . .*" and the women answered: "*Jesum Nazarenum crucifixum quaerimus.*" The angel then told them that Christ was not in the tomb, that He had arisen as He had foretold and the angel further asked them to go and announce the news. The Marys did so, whereupon a solemn *Te Deum* was sung.

Little by little this insignificant dramatic action acquired further characters: that of the apothecary from whom the Marys bought their ointments and even that of Christ who appears to Mary Magdalene, lamenting and weeping by the sepulchre after the departure of her two companions. Mary Magdalene then is the last to leave and tells the disciples the great news.

In the course of time other scenes were added — the scene with the apothecary who acquires an assistant was acted independently and subsequently it developed into a farce — other episodes from the life of Jesus were appended till the greater part of the Bible was dramatised.

This, however, would have been the beginning of another large chapter on extensive religious cycles which were no longer acted in the church, but outside in the square, and in which large numbers of lay actors participated.

30

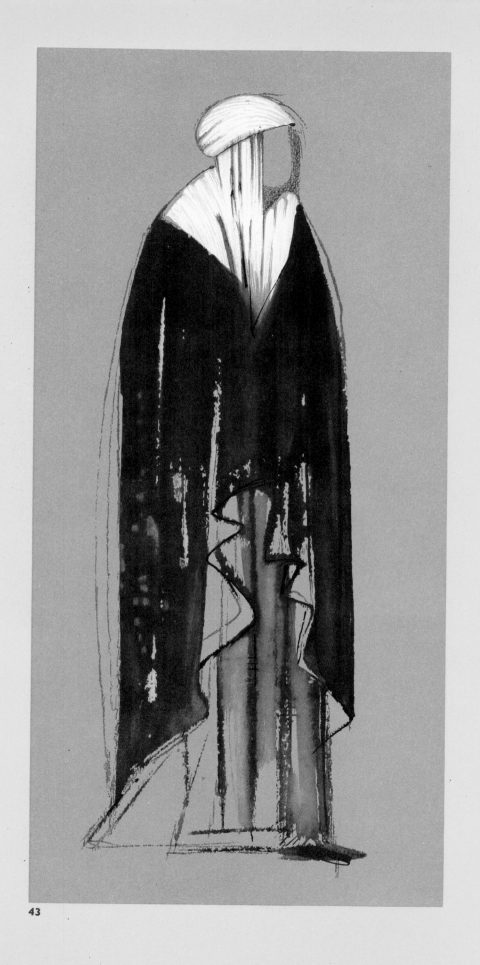

43

44

45

46

47

48

49

50

51

51 **Romeo**
52 **Juliet**
53 **Capulet**
54 **Mercutio**
55 **Benvolio**
56 **Lady Capulet**
57 **Tybalt**
58 **Nurse**
59 **Juliet**

Designs by Zdena Kadrnožková

WILLIAM SHAKESPEARE

Romeo and Juliet

To this day there may be found in Verona the tomb in which Romeo and Juliet are said to have died. This real, historical event of great love and joint death is said to have occurred at the beginning of the 14th century. Of course, objective historians, always distrustful of sentimental love-stories, assure us that it never happened. Be it as it may — even if the story did really happen, history and hard facts have proved to be less powerful than their artistic rendering.

If it was desired to enumerate all the works inspired by this tragic happening the list would be endless and never completely finished. Up to the end of the 16th century, that is to say before Shakespeare had written it, there existed a large number of works in prose, poetry, even drama, the heroes of which were Juliet Capulet and Romeo of the House of Montague. Some of these were known to Shakespeare and no doubt he was inspired by the famous story of the Italian Renaissance writer, Matteo Bondello, put into English verse by Arthur Brooke under the title of *Tragical History of Romeus and Juliet*.

It is a fact that this story was known to educated Elizabethans. Shakespeare's drama, however, made it immortal, which is more than writers of lesser genius were able to accomplish. Romeo and Juliet have become a symbol, even for people who have not read Shakespeare's drama; their story became universal property. It is constantly revived by all nations, at all times and in many forms.

Shakespeare's *Romeo and Juliet* is the finest play about love ever written. Lessing, reviewing one of Voltaire's plays, said that only Shakespeare had the power to write a work about love — the others are mere gallantry. Perhaps this criticism seems exaggerated and in the heat of discussion it sounds harsh — but can anything really compete with this *Romeo and Juliet*?

53

54

55

56

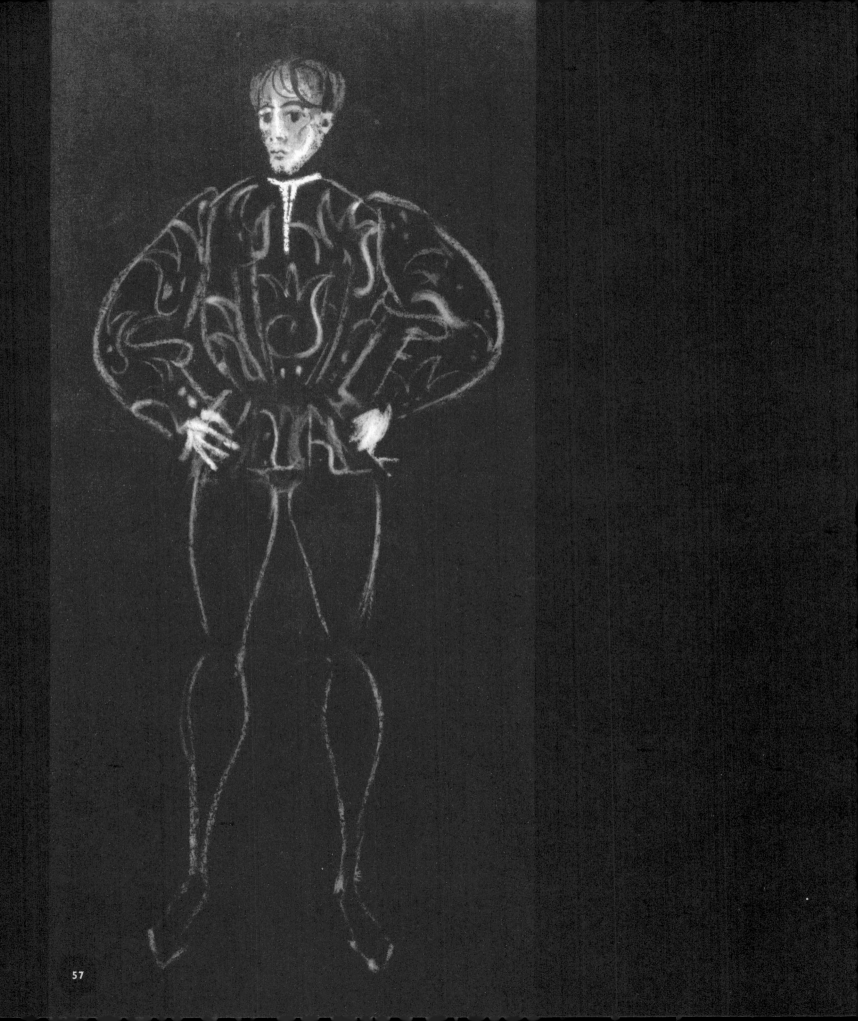

Designs by František Tröster

RICHARD WAGNER

Die Meistersinger von Nürnberg

When Richard Wagner was twenty-four years old, he encountered at Nuremberg the still lively tradition of local master-singers: the respectable master craftsmen of various guilds had fought annually for several centuries for the victorious laurel of the master-singer. That experience remained well imprinted on the composer's memory.

When years after he was composing in *Tannhäuser* the scene of the contest of singers at Wartburg, he relived the experience from his youth and began to occupy himself with the idea of creating a kind of comic counterpart to this situation as well as a whole opera. Thus the powerful operatic work *Die Meistersinger von Nürnberg*, in three acts, began to originate.

Wagner, librettist and composer in one person, introduces on the stage a young nobleman, Walter von Stolzingen, and lets him fall in love with Eva, the daughter of an esteemed Nuremberg burgher and recognised master-singer, Vitus Pogner, on the very St John's Eve, just before the day of the singing contest, and faces him right away with a very difficult task: the goldsmith Pogner, as a matter of fact, has publicly promised his lovely daughter to the master-singer who wins the forthcoming contest. Poor Walter, whose heart overflows with unfeigned passionate feeling, does not know the strict rules — since he learns singing only from the winged creation and from the works of the renowned Walter von der Vogelweide — has not much chance of success: at his first attempt Beckmesser, the malicious scrivener, who desires Pogner's daughter, registers a multitude of mistakes, so that the zealous adept fails disgracefully in front of the masters' assembly. One voice only is cast in his favour: it is from the most respected master — namely from Hans Sachs, the shoemaker-poet. Sachs also prevents the humiliated and disillusioned Walter from rashly eloping with Eva and the next day helps him to achieve the desired victory.

Thus the opera ends with an exalted apotheosis of Hans Sachs, personifying the noble behaviour of the Nuremberg Masters who fostered the prosperity and fame of art. That art which — to quote Lessing — canlby-pass invented rules whenever it pleases.

60

61

62

63

64

65

66

67

68

69

70

71

72

73

74

75

76

77

78

79

80

81

82

83

WILLIAM SHAKESPEARE

Richard III

Modern critics consider that the tragedy on King Richard III originated approximately in 1592; it is certain that this drama is a direct sequence of the preceding trilogy on Henry VI — assuming in addition its fairly detailed knowledge. As in the trilogy of the preceding works, *Richard III* depicts the history of bloody wars — they lasted a whole hundred years — between the White Rose of York and the Red Rose of Lancaster, the wars which in the end literally destroyed a great part of the English nobility. The foreign spectator, however, knows today only a fraction of this involved history, a few summary sentences or a mere marginal remark — which was mentioned during his school lessons on history, and if, in addition, he is unequipped — as in ninety-nine per cent of cases — with a knowledge of the preceding trilogy, he will not understand many allusions and even personalities. The theatres which occasionally introduce *Richard III* feel it their duty to check this muddle by extensive historical explanations, tabular summaries of dates, names and events and even graphically demonstrate the genealogy of the two decisive houses, both of which are represented in this play. A lack of knowledge of historical facts, however, does not prevent the ordinary spectator understanding this work of Shakespeare: the details may escape him but not its substance. Hundreds of thousands of spectators of the most varied nationalities have seen the film by Sir Laurence Olivier; they did not obtain any

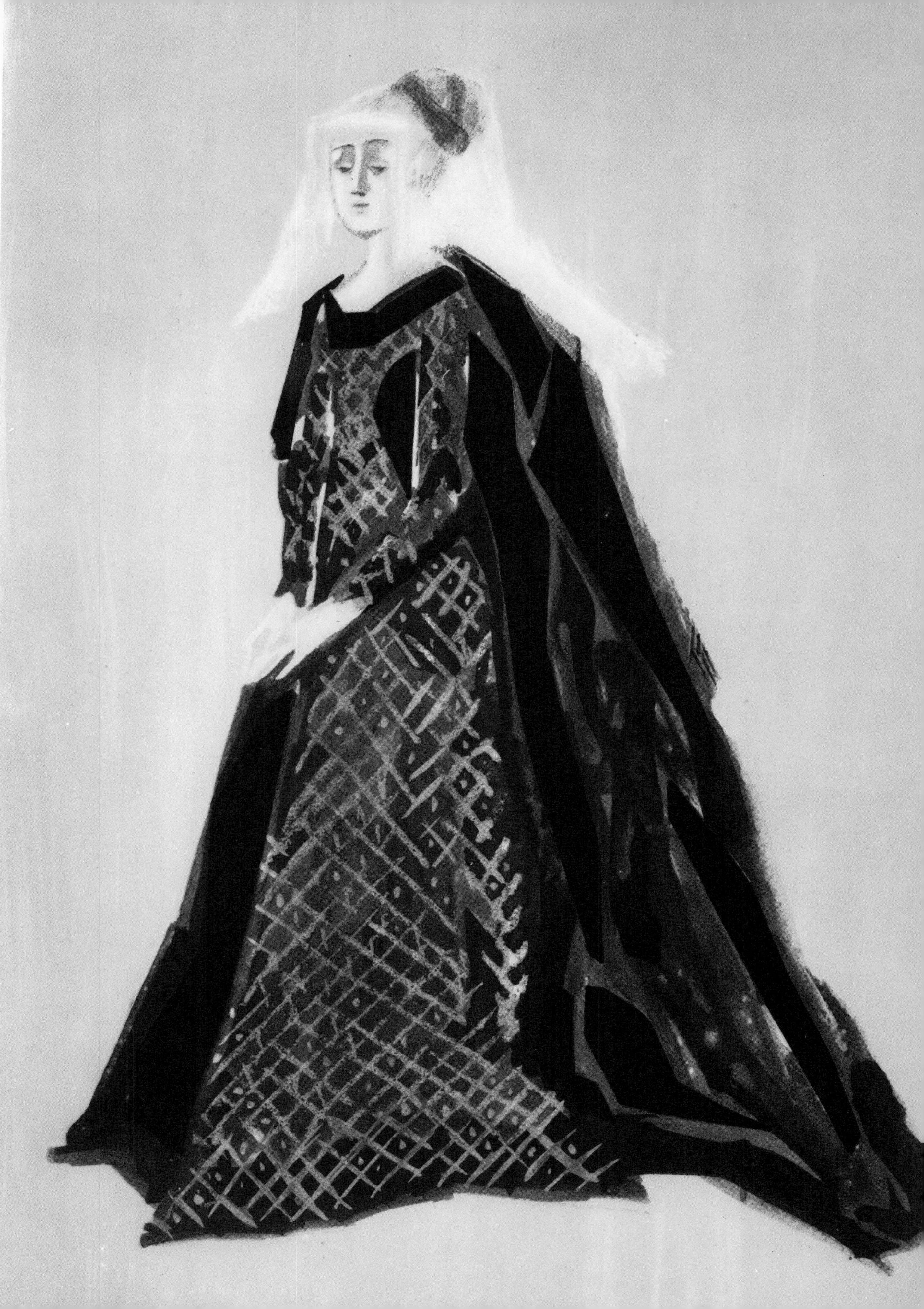

85

86

50

87

instruction and most of them did not know practically anything about the wars of the two roses. All the same they left the performance not confused but deeply moved. This is due, of course, not exclusively to the outstanding acting of Sir Laurence and his partners but to Shakespeare himself.

The fact that the tragedy on King Richard III represents a certain breach, in the attitude towards historical subjects, or to put it more accurately, the beginning of what we call the Shakespearean attitude, is probably the main point.

Richard III, as a matter of fact, is no longer a drama of events but of personalities and especially of one leading figure. In this it is different from the preceding trilogy, the standard of which is not strikingly above the current average of period chronicle plays. Only the most die-hard Shakespearians can affirm that *Henry VI* would deserve special attention were it not known that it was written by Shakespeare.

PIERRE CORNEILLE
Le Cid

About 1637 there was a saying in Paris "*Beau comme le Cid*". It was a short time after the first performance of the masterpiece of French classical drama, the tragi-comedy of the lawyer Pierre Corneille which was first applauded by everybody and which was later the object of a literary quarrel between the old school and the modernists (*La Querelle des Anciens et des Modernes*).

The history of the drama knows no other period where creative genius was so cramped by firm rules and conventions as the era of the reign of "The Sun King" Louis XIV. There existed many such rules and they were embodied in the famous didactic poem *L'Art poétique* by the theoretician Boileau. He is remembered especially by his law of the three unities of time, place and theme, derived from the drama of antiquity. Only one theme had to be developed without secondary episodes, the play had to take place in one locality, and the action was to be confined to one day. The least reasonable request was the last one — and even then attempts were made to reduce the time limit to a mere eight hours!

This did not, however, bother the dramatists who confined within one day so many actions that in reality they would take a whole week to happen. Unmindful of logic they strove only to obey the rule.

Let us now see how Corneille observed this rule and what occurred "in the course of a single day" in his drama. It is a conflict between love and honour experienced by the young Don Roderigo, surnamed The Cid for his valour in the war with the enemies of Spain.

93

94

95

96

97

98

60

The love of Roderigo and Chimène is about to have a happy ending, the lovers are of equal birth and their parents have given their consent to the marriage — were it not for an unfortunate incident which all at once upsets their plans. The hot-tempered Don Gomez, father of Chimène, still in his prime, insults and strikes the father of Roderigo, an old man who is hardly able to hold his sword. The father entreats his son to do his duty and avenge him. Roderigo realises that he risks the loss of Chimène's love but his honour does not permit any other choice. A duel takes place in which Roderigo kills Don Gomez. The unhappy Chimène is torn between her love for, and her equally passionate hate of, the man who has killed her father — and she asks for his death. Roderigo wants at first to leave this world of his own free will but his father persuades him to seek death — or glory — on the battlefield. Roderigo, The Cid, returns from the battle alive and famous for having won for Spain a great victory over the Moors. Again Chimène obstinately refuses to marry the murderer of her father; here intervenes the wise decision of the King Philip II who joins the hands of the two lovers on condition that Chimène will have a year to forget her father's death before celebrating her marriage. Love will thus have triumphed at last.

The stiff ideals of honour at any price and the cruel vengeance of insult are wholly different in character from those of the present generation. This frigid tragedy is now very rarely seen on the stage. But when it is successfully produced, then it is an unforgettable experience. Our recollection of the handsome, youthful Cid of the late Gérard Philippe brings to a close our appreciation of Corneille's tragi-comedy *Le Cid*.

91 **Chimène**
92 **Leonore**
93 **Don Arias**
94 **Don Sancho**
95 **Don Gomes**
96 **Don Rodrigo**
97 **Elvire**
98 **Dona Urraque**

Designs by Zdena Kadrnožková

99

Designs by Jan Skalický

Don Juan

Romeo and Juliet has already convinced us how some dramatic — and in general literary — figures return to life as definite types and how even their names serve for the designation of the predominant quality which they have so characteristically embodied. It is possible to mention a number of other examples. If you say of someone that he is a Hamlet, you obviously do not mean that he must avenge his father's death, but that he is simply a hesitating and indecisive man; if you call another one a Don Quixote, you do not want to say that he is an impoverished nobleman but are gently pointing out to him that he is a silly fool who vainly fights with poor weapons for futile or inaccessible ideals; as a matter of fact the psychoanalysts have called certain complexes by the names of Oedipus and Electra.

No figure of the drama, however, has become so firmly rooted as Don Juan. You can call someone a Don Juan with little praise or even with derogation but it will always be understood that you mean a philanderer or conqueror of women's hearts — in spite of the fact that a good number of writers and especially dramatists have tried to prove that the problem of Don Juan was not so unequivocal.

It is worth mentioning that this legendary Don Juan has embodied right from the beginning of his history more than a mere licence in erotic life: he represented a rake, atheist and blasphemer. This was the case in numerous folk tales as well as oral tradition of the haughty Spanish nobleman who did wrong till the Devil came for him and carried him away — which was also in substance the case when Don Juan was the hero of a really artistic work: the drama by Tirso de Molina *The Blasphemer of Seville*; this drama served also as a direct model for Molière's famous work which, however, as regards the conception of the titular hero, is absolutely independent of the Tirso play. It is a new conception.

In what does Molière's contribution consist? It is not easy to answer this question briefly. Molière's *Don Juan* has been a hard nut to crack for literary as well as theatrical theory; agreement has been reached that it is a case of a fully human figure and, therefore, a complicated one. Some voices drew attention to its internal lack of integrity — even two different personalities in one were mentioned. It is certain, however, that the renowned Juan's philandering plays only a partial role in Molière's rendering.

Molière's *Don Juan* is a figure of a great eccentric individualist who, on the one hand, does not recognise any secular or ecclesiastical authority — and on the other abounds in the worst possible life practice: namely false morals, hypocrisy. He is throughout an anti-social character who neither respects any propriety nor responsibility resulting from it.

Simultaneously, more than one of this freethinker's opinions sounds quite agreeably to our ears — and similarly it is impossible to deny Juan his personal courage. It is a strange personality of its kind, a man of unusual qualities — using his abilities and strength only for his own benefit, regardless of others — and against them.

Molière, as may be seen from our remarks, attempted to a certain extent to rehabilitate Don Juan: beginning with Molière's drama *Don Juan*, he ceased to exist as a typical villain and began in innumerable further works to come to life as an interesting type of man of a certain definite conception of life and attitude towards society. Nevertheless, neither Molière nor anybody since has removed that sobriquet which has been bestowed on Don Juan by popular tradition.

100

102

103

104

105

106

107

108

109

ALEXANDER PORPHYREVITCH BORODIN

Prince Igor

The history of the conclusion of the opera on Prince Igor is the story of a great and genuine friendship.

Alexander Porphyrevitch Borodin was not a musician by profession. His real profession was quite ordinary — and going by it, it would seem that Borodin and music were miles apart: the composer of *Prince Igor* was, as a matter of fact, a professor of chemistry, and music was only his hobby, but a hobby he loved heart and soul. Professor Borodin had composed a number of orchestral as well as chamber works, but the composition of one work was especially dear to him.

He conceived the idea to compose an opera on the heroic past of his nation, a monumental work, celebrating his country's heroism, integrity and desire for freedom, an apotheosis of the great impersonal goals for which man is willing to sacrifice his life. Prince Igor, the hero of the medieval song of Igor's Army, was one of the oldest and most valuable relics of Russian literature.

Borodin's *Prince Igor* is a story about the hero departing for his battle against Polovtsy's armed forces which threaten his country, about his love for his wife Jaroslavna whom he entrusts to the care of the treacherous Prince Galicki, who, taking advantage of the absence of Igor, attempts to seize the Government; the story further relates how the defeated Igor in captivity longs to return to his country and to regain his freedom, how he finally succeeds, is received with great joy by his loyal people and how he prepares himself for the retaliatory fight.

Opera as the "great genre" very often uses historical subjects, especially those where two nations fight each other. Into such a fight there is usually squeezed, for instance, an intimate love theme, as we have seen in *Aida*. Our case is different. In this opera there are in the balance first of all impersonal ideals — the destinies of individual figures, of the leading hero especially, are dealt with only in connection with them. Borodin worked a full seventeen

110

111

112

113

114

115

116

69

years on his great task and death interrupted his work. His work remained unfinished — the finale was missing and the overture was not written at all. Then Borodin's friends, Rimsky-Korsakov and Glazunov, relegated their own work and concentrated on the completion of *Prince Igor*. For instance, Glazunov, for whom Borodin had played the intended overture frequently, relied on his exceptional memory and wrote it down himself.

Rimsky-Korsakov and Glazunov were the first to recognise the importance of this magnificent torso.

117   119

118

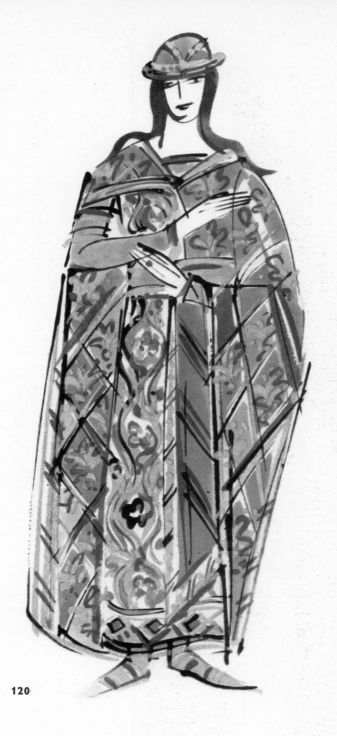

120

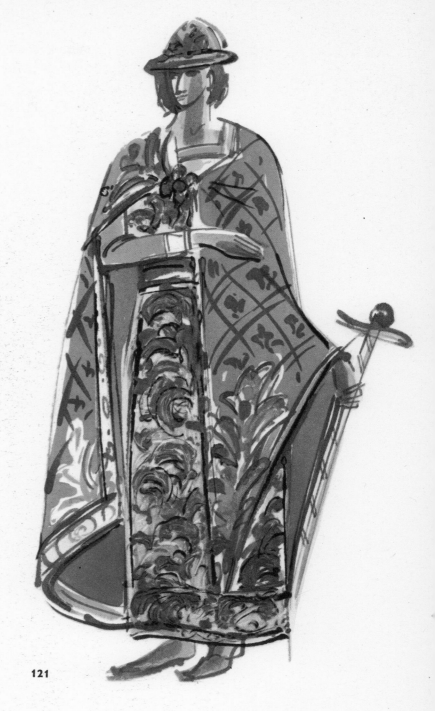

121

MODEST PETROVITCH MUSSORGSKY

Boris Godunov

Every nation which loves music has its truly national operas. The Russians have especially two: Borodin's *Prince Igor*, and *Boris Godunov* by Modest Petrovitch Mussorgsky. While the first of them is particularly festive, heroic and with apotheosis — *Boris Godunov* is an especially dramatic opera. While the hero of the former is an individual, a ruler, Prince Igor, the hero of the latter is the Russian people. Their destiny is here in play, their destiny is jeopardized by genuine as well as false czars and powerful boyars. It is not by chance that this work by Mussorgsky literally abounds in masterly composed mass scenes.

Today, after a lapse of some years, one can say that the plot of this monumental work begins where the grandiose film of S. M. Eisenstein, *Ivan the Terrible*, ended or should have ended. The Czar of all Russia had held the reins of government in iron hands and his throne was occupied by his son, the weakling Fyodor. The powerful nobility, the boyars whose power Ivan succeeded in temporarily breaking, again came forward, instead of Ivan a boyar council ruled with the Czarina's brother Boris at the head, and when Fyodor died, the boyars elected him as successor. The Czar left a second direct descendant, his younger son Dimitri who, however, was murdered — according to our information it was Boris who was mainly responsible for this murder. The elected successor hesitates to occupy the throne — but the boyars force the people to beg him to do so. Boris finally gives his consent. Thus begins the government of a Czar whose hands are soiled with the innocent blood of a child.

Boris governs for six years, sincerely trying to rule justly, but has neither the confidence of the people nor of the boyars, the shed blood burdens his conscience, while in the country resistance to him is growing. The fight for the throne is affected by a report that in Lithuania an usurper has appeared, the monk Grigori Otrepiev, who poses as Ivan's younger son, and whom the insurgents and Boris's opponents willingly accept as a figurehead.

123

124

125   126   127   128   129

The days of Boris Godunov's rule are numbered. At the Kremlin the boyars meet to take council on how to accept the usurper. This session is interrupted by the arrival of the already almost insane Boris, haunted by the vision of the slain Dimitri, who designates his son as the successor, imploring him to rule justly and to beware of the boyars — and dies.

In the meanwhile the impostor Dimitri is approaching. The opera culminates in a great scene of his meeting with the people: when the people realise that the first thing Dimitri does is to back a boyar who, although he was a Boris supporter, was all the same a nobleman — they disperse disillusioned and filled with dark forebodings.

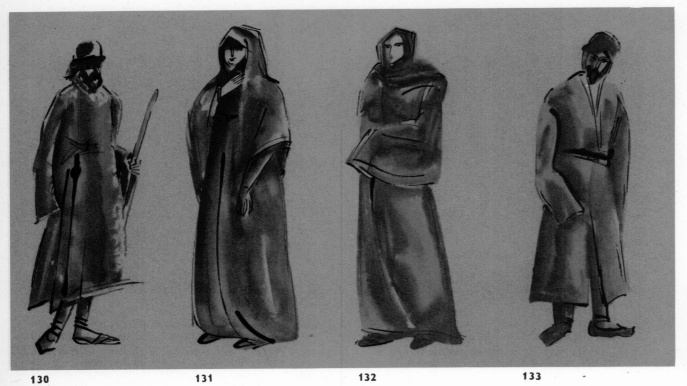

130   131   132   133

134

Designs by Ladislav Branč

135

136

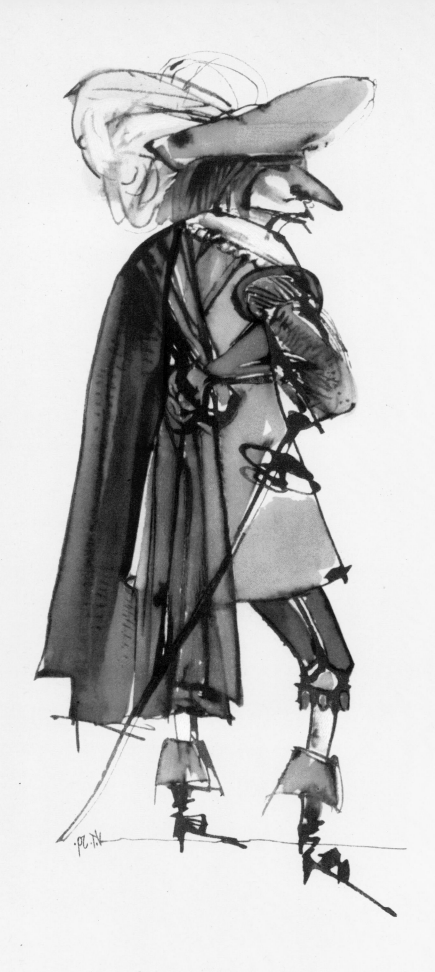

EDMOND ROSTAND

Cyrano de Bergerac

After the *première* of Cyrano in 1898 the French critics were extremely enthusiastic. Francis Sarcey, one of the leading critical spirits of that time, wrote: "We have now a real dramatic poet, a man with a gift. And the fact that this dramatic author is of French origin makes me all the happier . . . He is unaffected, clear, has movement and restraint, all the qualities characteristic of our race. How fortunate! How fortunate!" he concluded emphatically.

Cyrano de Bergerac arrived in good time. It appeared when the French theatre-goers were saturated by naturalistic and didactic plays, when they were tired of the giddy symbolism which on the stage wears out so quickly, and when they longed for a genuine, exciting theatre and dreamt of theatrical poesy. Rostand's Cyrano came on the scene as if timed. That animated whirl of events, passionate feeling, knightly self-denial, of love stormily manifested till beyond the grave and again of love hidden as far as the grave, was so theatrically dazzling, those Rostand Alexandrines sounded so agreeably to French ears that they took the wind from the sails of the most stubborn sceptics. They did not permit grain to be separated from chaff, depth from gilded surface, feeling from sentimentality, truth from faked illusion.

And what a period was revived in Rostand! The period of the greatest brilliance of the French kingdom, to which even the most diehard republicans were not indifferent, the period of a great upsurge of theatrical culture, the period of the legendary musketeers. How touching was the fate of Cyrano — that ugly man with noble soul, that knight without fear and without reproach, who cherished an unsoiled shield above all, who knew how to despise worldly fame, to love so loyally and discreetly, and oh, so splendidly! And to clothe all these brilliant qualities in scintillating words and magnificently composed tirades!

It did not matter at all that *Cyrano de Bergerac* by Rostand in no way advanced the development of French drama, not to mention world drama — that it was altogether a return to the past and a revival of ancient glory. *Chantecler*, the more valuable and original work by Rostand, did not by far achieve such a success — although the joyful acceptance of the older *Cyrano* had prepared the best ground for it. When the wave of enthusiasm fell — and it did not last very long — critical analyses discovered all the weakness of Rostand's work. One thing, however, no one could deny his work: namely a genuine theatricality. This has not evaporated until the present day.

Thus Rostand's *Cyrano* returns to the stage whenever the contemporary theatre suffers that most mortal disease: boredom.

138

139

140

143

144

145

146

Designs by Vladimír Tesař

147

148

149

MOLIERE *Le Malade Imaginaire*

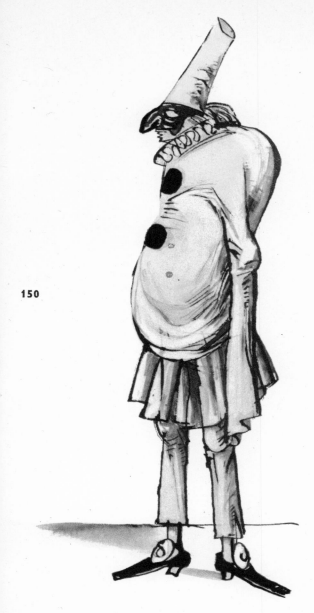

150

151

The last years of Molière's life were sad. He was pursued by poverty, in the course of a few years his son, then his wife, his second son and a close friend died. On the top of everything Molière contracted a disease for which there was no known remedy at that time: tuberculosis. In 1672 the King ordered from him an entertaining comedy-ballet, something on the lines of *Le Bourgeois Gentilhomme*. Molière gladly complied with his wish. He wrote the comedy *Le Malade Imaginaire*, which was played for the first time before the King at Versailles, which was very successful and in February 1673 was introduced to the Parisian public, again with outstanding success.

The fourth and the last performance of this play during the playwright's life took place on February 17th, 1673. Molière played, as usual, the title role of the hypochondriac Argan. Eye-witnesses later remembered that he played impressively, that he 'died' as never before. It appeared that he did not heed the advice of his friends who had known his state of health and seen how he was literally disappearing before their eyes. Molière did not obey. He did not want the performance to be cancelled and that his troupe — which was

152

facing bankruptcy in any case — should suffer another blow. He played with the utmost effort and put all his art into the play. He could not, however, endure the tension. In the closing ballet scene he fainted and it was necessary to carry him to the dressing-room. There he suffered a haemorrhage. He received no medical attendance, only a sister of mercy was present. Two priests refused to come and administer extreme unction: they refused to visit an actor and atheist, the author of the entirely disreputable *Tartuffe* and *Don Juan*. Excommunication and hate by the church pursued Molière to the grave: the Archbishop forbade the priests to officiate at the funeral ceremony and to bury the deceased in consecrated soil. Molière's companions appealed to Louis XIV himself, who took steps on behalf of his favourite actor. The church authorities, however, even then did not give way altogether — Molière

153

154

155

156

had to be buried in the dark and the ceremony had to be as simple and unobtrusive as possible.

The comedy of a sick man who is actually hale and hearty was the last work of the dangerously ill Molière. Molière certainly to the last minute did not believe that he was so seriously ill — in that respect he was mistaken — and simultaneously in this comedy was settling accounts with the surgeons who, as a matter of fact, did not know how to help him, prescribing for him medicaments hardly more effective than those which Monsieur Argan received from the apothecary Fleurant: and in this respect he was undoubtedly right. Life played him a grotesque, bad comedy, in which Death had the last word.

Designs by Vladimír Tesař

157

The Marriage of Figaro

Neither *Twenty Years After* nor *Le Vicomte de Bragelonne* can compare with the original *Three Musketeers*: sequels to popular works are usually weaker and result in the author being accused of commercialism. There are, however, exceptions — as is shown by the two plays by Pierre Augustin Beaumarchais, *Le Barbier de Séville* and *Le Marriage de Figaro* in which both the plot and the chief characters form a sequence, while the second play — the continuation — is even better than the first.

A critic wrote about Beaumarchais that by his *Marriage of Figaro* he accomplished more for the revolution than if he had staged a revolt. It seems exaggerated but it is true. *The Marriage of Figaro* had been forbidden in Paris for some years and when it was finally released in 1784, merely five years before the French Revolution, its stormy first night was cheered by the Third Estate. It was the same violent outburst of feeling as the explosion which several years later wrecked the walls of the Bastille. The spirit of this work, its ideals of democracy and liberty were namely identical with the slogans of the Revolution.

158

159

160

161

162

163

164

165

This famous *première* struck a light which like a flash of lightning leapt over the frontiers of France. *The Marriage of Figaro* inspired young Mozart who was not yet thirty at that time and as early as on the 1st of May, 1786, the first night of this opera-buffa took place in Vienna.

The libretto was written for Mozart by Lorenzo da Ponte — and according to the custom then prevailing operas were sung at the Vienna Court Theatre in the "classical opera language" — in Italian. The public understood little, pretended to understand more, and that was fortunate, otherwise who knows whether the *première* would have taken place at all?

This assumption is confirmed by the fact that when it was translated into German, the work was immediately banned from the stage.

Nevertheless the librettist had done his best to leave out political satire, especially the plebeian attack of Beaumarchais' comedy on the aristocracy; Figaro's famous monologue from the beginning of Act IV, in which Figaro compares his life with that of Count Almaviva, was left out in this version. Untouched remained Figaro's behaviour and his deeds which clearly indicate his — and Beaumarchais' — attitude. And Mozart's music fully reflected this democratic spirit.

Thus *The Marriage of Figaro* became not only an eternal proof of Mozart's musical genius but also of his civic courage and progressiveness.

167

166

Designs by Oldřich Smutný

RICHARD BRINSLEY SHERIDAN

The School for Scandal

An Englishman who reads the programme of the list of actors of *The School for Scandal* knows at once what kind of people play in this comedy: names like Surface, Teazle, Snake, Backbite or Sneerwell are sufficiently eloquent, justifying the title. Such "nomina-omina" or "speaking" names have, of course, occurred in dramatic literature down the ages; to find their origin one would have to go back as far as the renowned Greeks or Romans. This antique practice is revived — it stands to reason on a universal scale — by classicism which is customary in comedy: occasionally similar nomenclature is encountered in cases when the persons are characterised by one prevailing quality — being a kind of living symbol of jealousy, avarice, prodigality, etc. They are not complete human personalities, they are imaginary figures — satires and caricatures. To reproach today their author for that which was then his intention would be futile and rather unfair.

We have, as a matter of fact, indirectly suggested that the Sheridan comedy is a satire, that the author looked at his contemporaries through a sharp magnifying glass which at multiple enlarging deforms in its way, as it lets one part monstrously excel — while suppressing the other ones which are no more in

171   172

173

the field of sight. Sheridan focused his attention on the human drones who from absolute lack of other employment and with a kind of sportsman's enthusiasm scandalise one another, and what they do not know, they invent; to put a spicy scandal into circulation is what matters.

This society is a kind of background for the play, the substance of which consists in revealing immoralities genuine as well as false, in the punishment of hypocrisy and the reward of sincerity. The decisive role in *The School for Scandal* is played by the two Surface brothers. The first one, Joseph, dispensing morals right and left, is joviality itself and is popular in "good society". The other appears to be the essence of iniquities, he shuns good society, preferring to drink with jolly companions and instead of moralising squanders the family fortune. These two young men and rivals in love (with the first one only simulated, with the other one real) are subjected to a test of genuineness by their rich uncle Oliver: the hypocrite Joseph is weighed and found wanting, the other one, on the contrary, is revealed as a young man with a good heart. The scoundrel is found out in the end and the good man is rewarded as it should be: with a lovely bride, a big dowry and the prospect of an even bigger inheritance.

175

176

174

177

178

179

180

CARLO GOLDONI
Servant of Two Masters

The Italian Renaissance gave birth in the sixteenth century to a characteristic type of popular theatre, later on called *Commedia dell' Arte*.

It was a theatre of masks, to put it better, of stable character types which were discerned by the spectators already at first glance by the costumes. There were among them Dottore, a lawyer of Bologna, merchant Pantalone of Venice, the boastful soldier Capitano — but especially a rich scale of servants and their partners in love as well as employment. Especially three standard servant types were always repeated: Arlecchino, who always muddled up his master's orders, the cleverer Brighella who on the other hand used to commit plenty of stupidities, and the eldest and wisest of them, Bulcinella.

Commedia dell' Arte was improvised; there were no fixed texts, for the most part the ablest actors invented a kind of draft libretto, a rough synopsis, which was filled with life by abundant imporvisations only in front of the public.

At first this theatre was a mirror of life of its kind, later on it became stale and was a ballast in the development of individual national cultures — as *commedia dell'Arte* then ceased to be a purely Italian affair; in a rather different form its types frequently occurred especially in France and Germany — and the new dramatic authors had to deal with it one way or another. In the case of unusual talents — such as Molière or Goldoni — it was achieved informally: in the creations of both authors we can follow a gradual development from the dependence on these types, corresponding to our times.

In the work of Carlo Goldoni, the greatest representative of Italian national comedy, it is possible to find such a clear milestone, marking the mentioned transition. It is Goldoni's first famous and today still popular comedy *Servant of Two Masters*, written in 1745.

The text which has been handed down to us is not literally identical with that according to which the famous comic Antonio Sacchi played for the first time in 1749. For this actor, accustomed to improvisation, the servant's role of Truffaldino who by mere chance had to serve two masters, was an occasion to display his brilliant store of jokes and hints, called *lazzi*. The traditional elements of the *Commedia dell'Arte*, however, are to be found not only in the performance of Goldoni's play: they are in the text itself. Even the motif of the killing of the bride's brother by the lover makes itself felt here, and among the persons encountered is Pantalon as well as Dottore.

Perhaps it is just the form flexibility of the *Servant of Two Masters*, offering enough possibility for the deployment of that eternal comic acting which is a guarantee of the vitality of Goldoni's comedy.

Designs by Jan Skalický

182

183

184

185

186

187

188   188

189   189

190   190

191   191

192   192

193   193

188   **Louise-Françoise Contat I**

189   **Anne-Lucie Philippe**

190   **Louise-Françoise Contat II**

191   **Gonehon**

192   **Félix-Hubert de Vintimille**

193   **Bernard-René Jourdan**

14th July

"If anyone desires to depict the whole," wrote Romain Rolland in the introduction to his drama *14th July*, "he cannot paint every wave but the wide sea. An impassioned truthfulness of the whole is more important than punctilious accuracy to detail."

14th July is a part of Rolland's intended cycle of plays on the Great French Revolution which, however, remained a torso. It is the third drama of this kind by Rolland — *Les Loups* and *Danton* preceding it — thematically, however, it is the introductory part of the planned cycle.

The plot of the drama taking place exactly on the 12th—14th July of the memorable year of 1789, can be expressed in a few words: the people of Paris riot, build barricades, attack the Bastille and conquer it. It is difficult to speak here at all of the leading dramatic figures as individuals — although on the one hand the great personalities of the Revolution, such as Robespierre, Desmoulins, Hoche or Marat are encountered here — and in the last act, in the courtyard of the renowned Parisian fortress prison, we become acquainted also with their opponents in the persons of the Governor of the Bastille, the commanders of the Swiss Guard and the French Invalides. As a matter of fact a collective — the Parisian people — is here the hero of this drama. It is really in the character and intention of this drama not to paint every wave but one wide sea. Although several detailed scenes imbued with originality, charm and wit are to be found here — such as the one in which Juliette, a Parisian child, carried on the back of Hoche, bearing the flag of truce, penetrates into the surrounded fortress as a dove with an olive branch of peace — the main emphasis is laid on the scenes where the mass of the people gets into revolutionary stride.

There was possibly no other choice if *14th July* was to be a play on the Parisian people and if it desired markedly to continue the interrupted tradition of the *Fêtes populaires*, folk festive plays with dance and music, by which during the reign of Revolution its victory was celebrated.

194   195   196

197   198   199

200   201   202

203   204   205

Designs by Vladimír Tesař

206   207   208

209   210   211

213

PETER ILYITCH TCHAIKOVSKY

Eugen Onegin

With the exception of a mere two works Tchaikovsky did not compose on any other theme but the Russian: in a letter addressed to the Czech lady translator of his libretto he wrote: "I know and understand only the Russian man, Russian girl and woman."

When he decided to express in music the powerful novel in verse by A. S. Pushkin he realized the difficulties connected with the chosen task — as a matter of fact, the critic Bielinsky called *Eugen Onegin* the encyclopedia of Russian life — and then gave his work a modest subtitle: *Lyrical Scenes*.

Indeed, Tchaikovsky's attitude to the material of *Onegin* is first of all lyrical. Owing to operatic transformation much of the content of the original work disappeared. This does not, of course, apply merely to the details of the plot — but especially to the characteristics of the persons. Eugen Onegin in this interpretation is above all a *blasé*, almost cynical young man while in the case

214

of Pushkin's novel he is to a certain extent quite sympathetic (actually it was
a kind of self-portrait). Vladimir Lensky is represented similarly simplified:
as an enthusiastic dreamer and idealist — while Pushkin did not hesitate to
invest him with an ironic sneer. Tatyana is the figure nearest to the composer's
heart: in the famous letter scene and then in the final duet with Onegin,
Tchaikovsky's music created a magnificent apotheosis of her moral purity and
steadfast character.

The composer succeeded in differentiating strikingly by musical means in a unique way between the two decisive milieux: the Larins' country house and worldly Petersburg. The key position is here occupied by the masterly ball scenes, which are the culminating point of. the first and second part of the opera. While at the first ball, given by the Larins on the occasion of Tatyana's birthday, where the bored Onegin actually provokes his friend Lensky to a duel — which ends for him so tragically — may be heard the traditional but cordial Mazurka and waltz — at the second Petersburg ball, the sophisticated couples dance to the rhythm of the formal, cold Polonaise. There Onegin's tired and gloomy eyes rest on an unknown beauty and after asking his friend, Prince Gremin, who she is, ascertains that this aristocratic lady of noble demeanour is the former dreamy, shy girl from a certain country seat, who had foolishly fallen in love with him at first glance and whose advances he had rejected — but this time it is he himself who succumbs to an obstinate, unbridled passion. In vain. With surprising fortitude Tatyana resists his outbursts. She remains faithful to her husband — and what is more, she remains faithful to herself.

215

216

217

Designs by Oldřich Smutný

218

219

220

NICOLAI VASSILYEVITCH GOGOL

The Inspector General

221

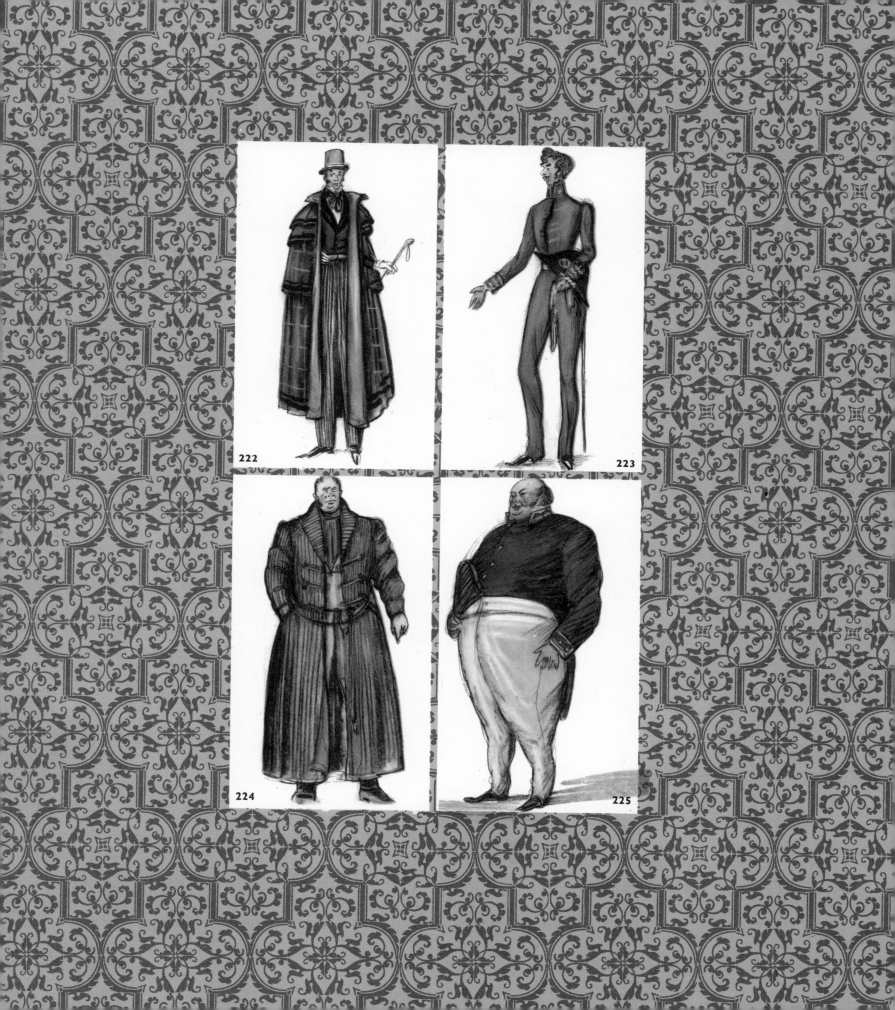

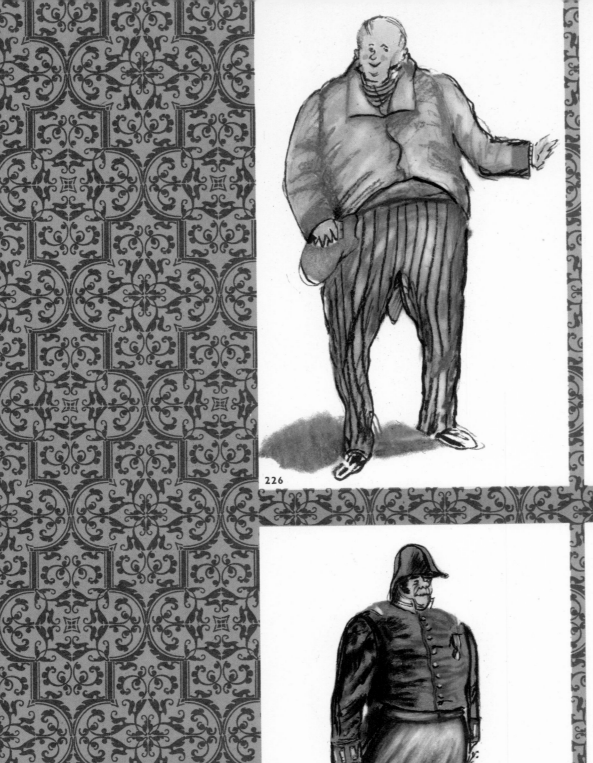

226

227

228

229

The young adepts of literature who proclaim that they would gladly write a novel — story — drama, if only they had a theme, are not to be laughed at for this reason. Even the greatest writers know such moments. Gogol wrote in October, 1835, an imploring letter to his friend Pushkin: "Have mercy on me and give me a theme, be it comic or not, only if it is a purely Russian anecdote. My hand itches to write a comedy just now . . . Have mercy on me, give me a theme; the spirit of the comedy will require five acts and I swear — it will be devilishly comic!"

Pushkin did not disappoint his friend. He offered him a short, three-line anecdote as follows: A man comes to a small gubernatorial town, whom the local population takes for an inspector general, trembling before him in fear, doing their best for him and throwing dust in his eyes. The man enjoys himself, then disappears and before the townspeople recover from this shock they receive a message that another inspector is on the way — this time the real one.

Gogol kept his word. He sat down and wrote. The comedy was completed as early as January of the following year and in April, 1836 had its *première* in Petersburg. The Tsar himself sat in the royal box, surrounded by his suite, and is said to have laughed merrily. If the play pleased the Tsar, it naturally also pleased others so that the *Inspector*'s success was guaranteed. The author, however, was not satisfied: neither with the actors, who had not played according to his wishes, nor with his own work. Against the former he could not do anything but at least he rewrote the play in its final shape, in which it is known today: the final wording of the *Inspector General* is from as late as 1842.

Gogol did not like it that everyone, headed by the Tsar, laughed and enjoyed themselves so heartily. Not in vain did he put in front of his play as a motto the Russian folk saying: "Do not blame the mirror for your ugliness."

230

A still more distinct intention made itself felt in the corrections and insertions of further versions. After the experience of the first night Gogol put into the mouth of the police director in the closing part of the play, at the moment when the whole auditorium is shaking with laughter at the gentlemen, with the director at their head, who have been deceived, several famous sentences which the actor usually shouts angrily into the audience: "What are you laughing at, hey? What are you laughing at? Laugh at yourself!"

Gogol wished to emphasise his intention "to collect in a heap all which is rotten in Russia ... and laugh at it once and for all". He hoped that the people would recognise themselves in the figures of his comedy — if not in that camarilla of small town jobbers and idiots, then perhaps at least partially in that false Inspector Khlestakov, a little man who poses as a great one. Let us be frank: how many of us do not resemble a little Khlestakov?

To provoke irresponsible laughter was not the aim of *The Inspector General*. Gogol certainly did not desire the people to stop laughing — but he did not like it when they laughed too carelessly, as if the action on the stage did not concern them. The laughter at the Inspector should have been the Gogolian "laughter through tears".

Designs by František Tröster

231

232

233

234

ALEXANDER NIKOLAIEVITCH OSTROVSKY

The Storm

On a summer afternoon when a storm is approaching, the heroes of the drama *The Storm* by Alexander Nikolaievitch Ostrovsky are seen on the banks of the river Volga. The inhabitants of the small town of Kalinov have gone for a Sunday walk — the Kabanov family among them: the rich merchant Marfa Kabanova, called Kabanikha, her son Tikhon and daughter-in-law Katya. Katya is a simple girl from a poor family who has married into a rich one: for love. She loved her husband and tries to do so even now — but she cannot respect him. Tikhon is fond of her in his own way but he is a weakling, indecisive and meek, in every respect under the influence of his mother who firmly holds the reins of the whole family, tyrannising Katya. Tikhon is unable to resist his mother and stand up for his wife, as the fear of his mother is much stronger then the feeling which binds him to his wife. He is a man who desires peace at any cost and who is willing to sacrifice everything in the interests of this imaginary peace.

Therefore he welcomes the fact that he is obliged to leave his home for a fortnight on account of business. He takes leave of his wife as his mother orders and Katya remains at home alone — with her recollections of the dreams of her childhood, the longing for a full life, lived side by side with a strong man who would support her and be worth her love. Now she knows that Tikhon is not the right one, realising that he is a man she does not love; she does her best to resist the temptation to meet another one who pleases her and professes to be in love with her. She does not resist. During the whole time Tikhon is away she meets Boris every evening. Then Tikhon returns — sooner than expected. No, no one will betray Katya that in his absence she was meeting a lover, and nothing would happen if . . . if Katya was different, if those meetings would be for her a mere flirtation or if she was satisfied with a short episode of fleeting happiness. Katya, however, does not belong to those people who are satisfied with little or those who

237

239

240

241

242

243

can simulate. First of all she becomes suspect on account of her strange conduct — then she confesses to her husband. Tikhon does not know what to say.

Again nothing would have happened and the storm might have been prevented but for Katya's rare purity and sense for truth, honour and her high morality. When Katya finds out that Boris is leaving, refusing to take her with him — as he is of a more practical turn of mind than she — she finds herself in a situation which for her has only one possible solution: suicide. She dies by jumping into the river Volga and above her corpse stands the weeping Tikhon with helplessly hanging arms.

After the *première* of this supreme work by A. N. Ostrovsky the public as well as the critics divided into two adversary camps. The conservative part indignantly refused it as an attack on the Government — the democratic part enthusiastically welcomed *The Storm* for the same reasons. Turgenev at that time wrote in a letter that "it is the most wonderful and grandiose work of the Russian talent, powerful and with perfect self-control" and later on Goncharov in a review for the Academy wrote: "Without being afraid of overstatement I can in all conscience say that our literature so far did not possess such a work … It assumes and will assume a leading place for its great classical beauty". A basic analysis of *The Storm* was written after its publication by N. A. Dobrolyubov, the highly talented Russian literary critic and a revolutionary democrat. In the title of his excellent essay he called Katya "a ray of light in the realm of darkness". This classical characteristic is so expressive that it cannot be improved upon.

235 Tikhon Ivanovich Kabanov
236 Marfa Ignatievna Kabanova
237 Kaya
238 Kudriash
239⎫
240⎭ Town's People
241 Varvara
242⎫
243⎭ Town's People

Designs by František Tröster

244

GEORGES BIZET

Carmen

Not only books but operas, too, have their destinies. Bizet's *Carmen* is known today even by those who have never in their life seen it in the theatre. Fragments are included in practically all wireless programmes of popular operas, and the most famous of them — the Toreador theme — is whistled by urchins in the streets.

All the same this opera, which is one of the most renowned and popular ones, was on its first night — at the very end of the composer's life — accepted by the Parisian public so coolly that it meant a failure. Bizet, although he believed in the value of his work, did not live long enough to obtain satisfaction. His *Carmen* left the ungrateful Parisian public and went round the world. It was a famous tour — and its return to Paris after eight years was triumphant.

What then was the cause of the initial failure? The reason was probably the libretto which was written by the experienced Meilhac and Halévy after the extensive novel by Prosper Mérimée. The refined Parisian public was used to choice works, supplied by the zealous producers of salon operas, and this work of Bizet appeared to them to be rough, loud and coarse. The curtain goes up — on the stage there is an ordinary factory — and then the stage is filled with a chorus representing factory girls. Or that common tavern on the outskirts of the town in the second act. In the last act again the awful crowd, filling the arena for the bull-fight, and all ending in a crude murder: the jealous Sergeant José stabs his gypsy sweetheart to death. And this Carmen — is she a regular operatic heroine?

How does the rehabilitated *Carmen* win the public today? Certainly already by the passionate southern hue, the jubilant, even gaudy richness in colour of its melodics as well as the skirts of the young Spanish girls who come forward on the stage in the first act — in their midst being that proud and challenging gypsy Carmen with an acacia twig in her teeth; by that wild dance whirl in the tavern where Carmen was hidden and found by Sergeant José who from love of her becomes a member of the smuggling gang — that romanticism of a dangerous enterprise, where lives are at stake; and again by that scintillating splendour of the finale, those dazzling costumes of the picadors, matadors, toreadors and banderilleros — and finally by that unusually effective finale, in which in the background of the stage sounds the jubilant song of the crowd, celebrating Escamillo's victory, while in the foreground Carmen is dying, slain by the hand of her rejected lover.

245 246 247

248

249

250

The unfailing success of this opera is guaranteed not only by the fact that Bizet's *Carmen* wins the spectator at first glance and at first hearing; the spectator with fine feeling is attracted in this work by something more substantial and deeper: namely the tragic fate of the woman who was too much of a woman, and who did not consider sufficiently the destructive force of erotic feeling.

251

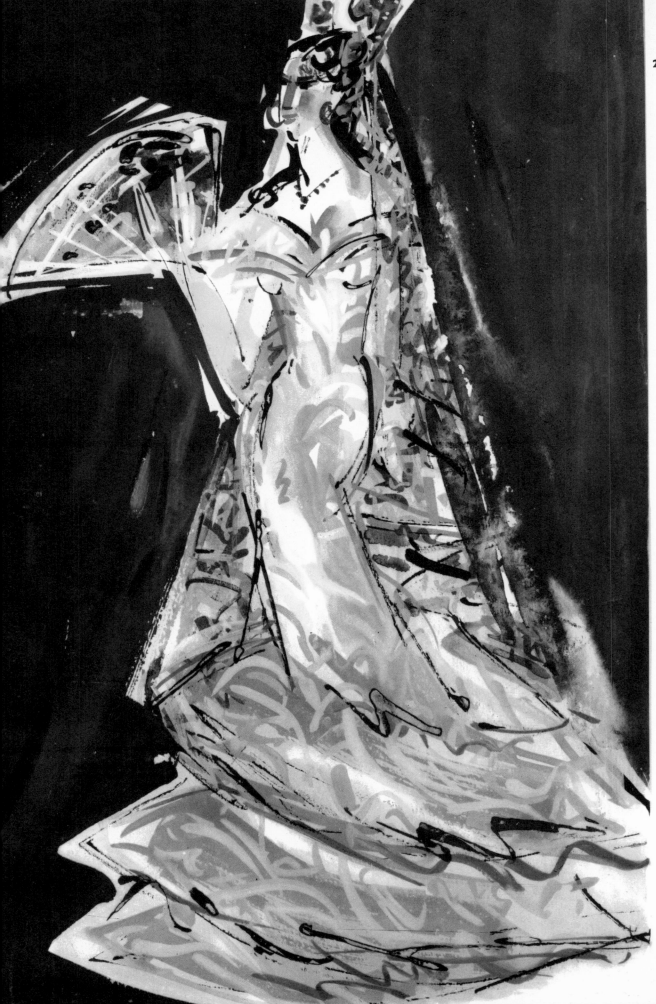

253

254

GIACOMO PUCCINI

Turandot

Very few composers literally abounded in an inexhaustible supply of melodics, very few knew so well how to stage an opera, and very few succeeded
in expressing by means of music feelings and passions with such suggestive
effectiveness. However much experts may have reproached Puccini for his incli-
nation to sentimentatily, exotism and drastic effects, even suggesting that he
tried unscrupulously to win the spectator's favour and please him at any cost—
all in vain; such a *Madame Butterfly* or *Turandot* always remain works which—
if suitably (i.e. expensively) produced — are an unfailing attraction for the
opera-going public; to introduce them in a good production in repertory
means to have full houses as well to be fully booked up — which, as an experienced American producer stated, never fails.

Experts may, therefore, proclaim ad infinitum that Puccini is not really
the most prominent of the modern or quite recent opera composers, that his
work does not represent the acme achieved in this genre and reproach him
for this or that: the public will have its say. As a matter of fact Puccini's
pleasing music, a certain sensationality of the motifs of his operas and the
scenic splendor with which they must be adorned, literally caress the ears and
eyes of the spectator.

Let us take, for instance, the subject matter of the composer's last opera,
performed as late as eighteen months after his death — in 1926. We have in
mind his second — "Chinese" — opera which, contrary to the first one, has
a fairy-tale motif: Princess Turandot.

Numerous dramas as well as operas have been written on this motif; up to
then the dramatic production by Carlo Gozzi, the successful contemporary

256

257

258

259

143

260   261

Designs by Ladislav Brančˇ

and more fortunate rival of Goldoni, was the best known, until the operatic execution of Giacomo Puccini beat it in popularity.

Let us hear the story of the Oriental fairy-tale in Puccini's rendering.

In front of the gates of the city of Peking a mandarin announces that any one who wishes to woo the beautiful princess Turandot must undergo a hard test: to solve her three puzzles — and if he does not guess, he will be executed. Shortly afterwards, as one of these daring young men is being led away to be executed, it so happens that among the spectators there is an unknown prince who, after getting a glimpse of the princess, falls head over ears in love with her. Heedless of warning he tempts his luck — with success. Turandot feels humiliated but the gallant prince makes her a generous offer: this time she will have to guess his name but without his former risk. The princess fails to guess, the prince wins and after a short peripetia love is the victor over wickedness and hatred — as it should be on the stage, so that the spectator as well as the booking-office are satisfied.

262

263

The Bartered Bride

After the first night of *The Bartered Bride* in 1866 the librettist Sabina declared: "Had I known what kind of music Smetana would compose, I would have produced a better libretto." The enthusiastic response to Smetana's second operatic work, surprised the composer himself, who accepted it as an incitement for further work. For Smetana the work on the score did not end with the opening night; he was further improving it, adding other numbers — for instance, he composed a splendid dance for the beginning of the third act. Thus as early as 1870 *The Bartered Bride* was completed in the form in which it is known today by the whole world.

Then, later, doubting voices made themselves heard to the effect that this time Smetana had not distinguished himself too much, that his work was shallow and without any obligation. Of course, Smetana did not intend at all to compose a complicated work, full of great ideas and passions. He wished simply to write a popular opera, accessible to the greatest possible number of the musical public, a work for the people's enjoyment. In that he more than succeeded.

Sabina wrote for him a simple story of the country journeyman Jeník who falls in love with Mařenka, the daughter of a landowner. This Mařenka, however, is promised to another young man, but Jeník finally outwits them all, winning his love and in addition the three hundred ducats which he received for giving up Mařenka to the son of Tobias Mícha: namely to himself. Smetana's music imbued these figures with life; the charming melodies of this smiling comic opera (opera-buffa) are full of typical Czech melodiousness and the whole work is a joyful acceptance of simple, loyal and sincere human feeling and folk wit.

A few years after the composer's death, that "too Czech opera" found its way to the whole world. The sceptical fears proved to be unfounded. The people understood the warm sentiment and optimism of this opera; at some places they even adapted it to conform to their conceptions. In the Smetana Museum in Prague there is a picture from a scene somewhere in South America: there Mařenka is in her national costume — and beside her on the village green palms are growing. We smile but do not laugh at it.

264

265

266

267

268

269

270

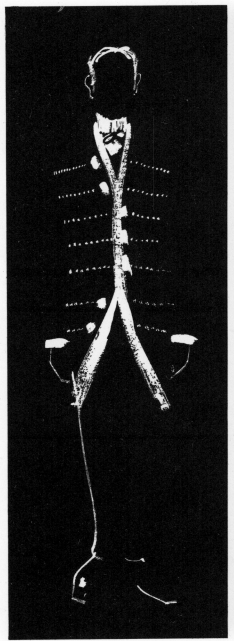

271   272

Designs by Jan Skalický

OSCAR WILDE

An Ideal Husband

It may be quite a subjective and inappropriate feeling but when reading the dramas by Oscar Wilde one must doubt what of that accumulation of brilliant wit, shabby sentiment, melodramatic would-be seriousness and moralizing should be taken seriously and the idea occurs whether those social comedies by Wilde, which for more than a half century have ideally satisfied the taste of the average spectator are not one great mystification by Oscar Wilde.

Let us take *An Ideal Husband*. It is some time before you begin to learn what the play is actually about, but till then you are excellently amused by Wilde's perfect sketches of unimportant people who talk a great deal but say nothing. Then your attention is absorbed by persons who must be taken seriously: Sir Robert Chiltern, Assistant Secretary for Foreign Affairs, a man honoured and respected in office as well as in society, his young wife Gertrude who does not excel in anything but honesty and purity, both, however, genuine, and as the last of this trio a certain Mrs Chevely who can be characterised as the very opposite of the collection of virtues of her schoolmate Gertrude — even stealing. It appears that Sir Robert also has a skeleton in the cupboard and is, therefore, blackmailed by Mrs Chevely; Gertrude wrings her hands, Sir Robert hesitates between position and honour, everything becomes very involved indeed, both sides alternatively having their ups and downs, until everything develops to general satisfaction: the bad woman is driven away, Sir Robert accepts the post of Secretary of State which a few minutes before he was rejecting on account of bad conscience, one home fire keeps again merrily burning and the other is just being kindled. A happy end according to all the rules.

Is it possible to believe that the witty Wilde could have written such a banal and dull end in all seriousness?

273

274

275

276

277

278

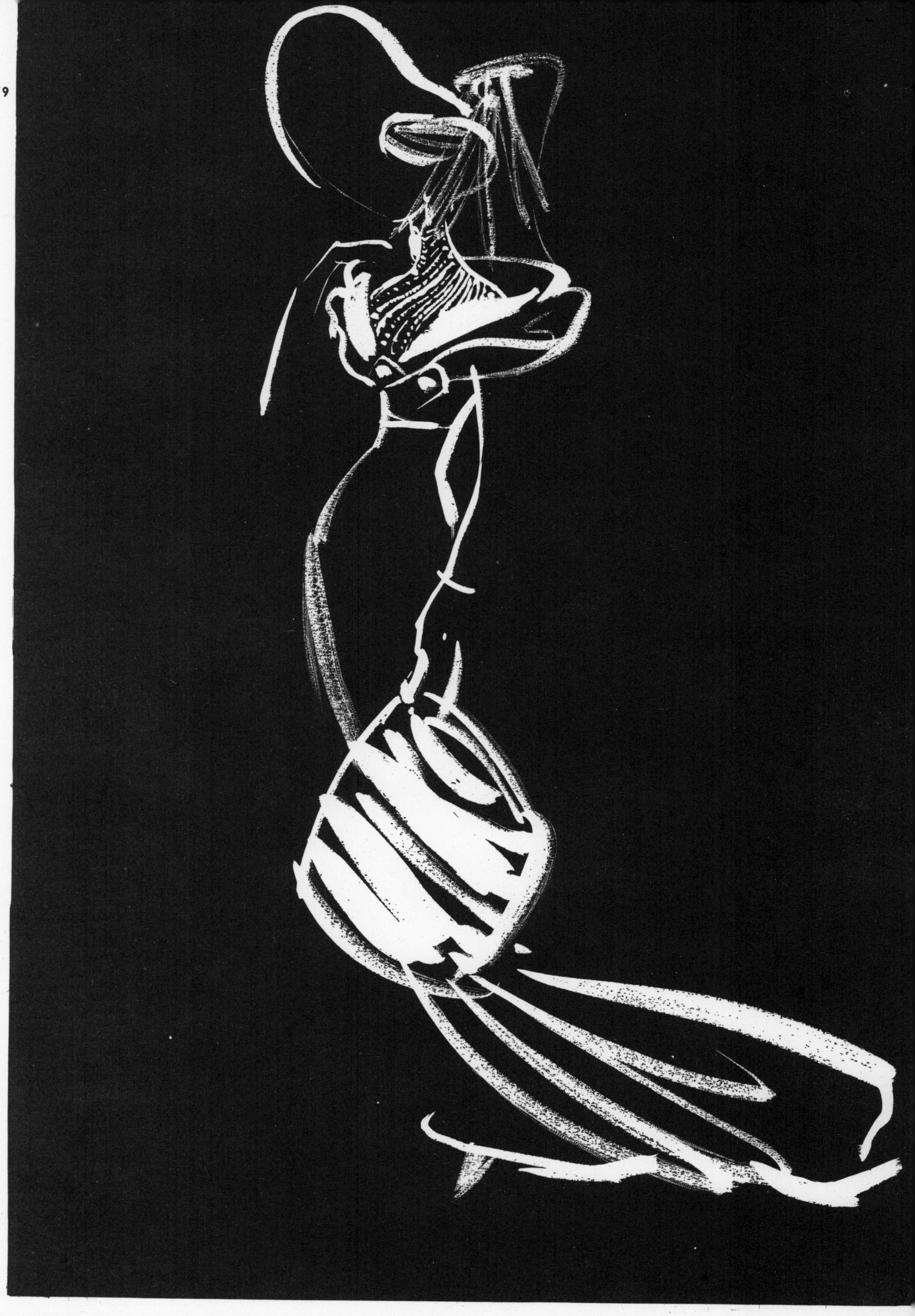

HENRIK IBSEN

Nora

In the last, third act of Ibsen's play, Nora says to her husband Helmer these grave words: "...Our home has only been a kind of doll's room with which the children play. I have been your wife but you have treated me as a puppet, as a plaything — just as when I used to be a doll of my father. And our children have again been my puppets... Such has been our marriage." This passage explains the rather unusual title of the drama—*The House of Dolls*.

Nora Helmer spent in this house a good many years of her life. She married a nice respectable man, bore him three children, and everything would have been in order even now but for that terrible shock, astounding recognition, the sense of which was explained in Nora's words. Nora found the moral courage to bring things to a head. She cannot live any longer in this atmosphere which has suddenly become unbearable: at the conclusion of the drama Ibsen's heroine decides to leave her husband, as well as her children.

That provocative conclusion was a gauntlet thrown in the face of society in which the woman's place and interests were defined by three conceptions: *Kinder, Küche, Kirche* — while any exception to these three K's was taboo. No wonder that the the first night and the book form of *The House of Dolls* incited far-reaching discussions not only Ibsen's own country but all over Europe. Even those who acknowledged Nora the right to leave her husband and live her own, independent life, could not reconcile themselves to the fact that Nora left her own children. For instance, the German performer of Nora refused to play this finale and turned to Ibsen with a request to change it. Ibsen hesitated a long time, then consented and altered the finale so that Nora cannot resist the sight of her sleeping children and decides to remain — on account of them. This conclusion may be psychologically more probable but the fighting credo of this play was considerably blunted as a result.

The several decades which separate us from the date of the *première* have certainly deprived *Nora* of a great deal of excitement: her problems are distant from ours. At its time, however, *The House of Dolls* was a *Zeitstück* in the best sense of the word.

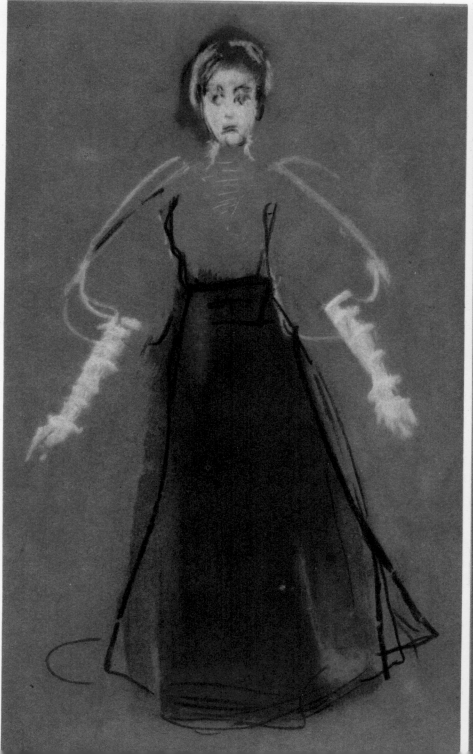

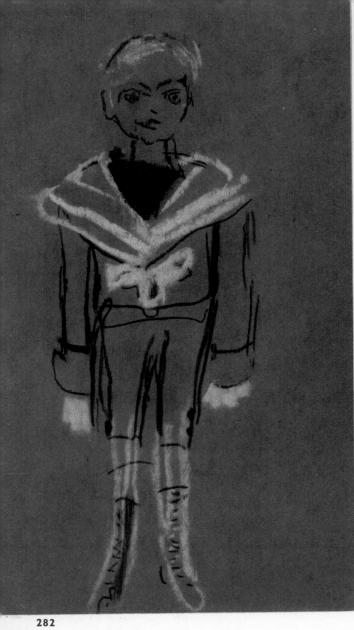

282

283

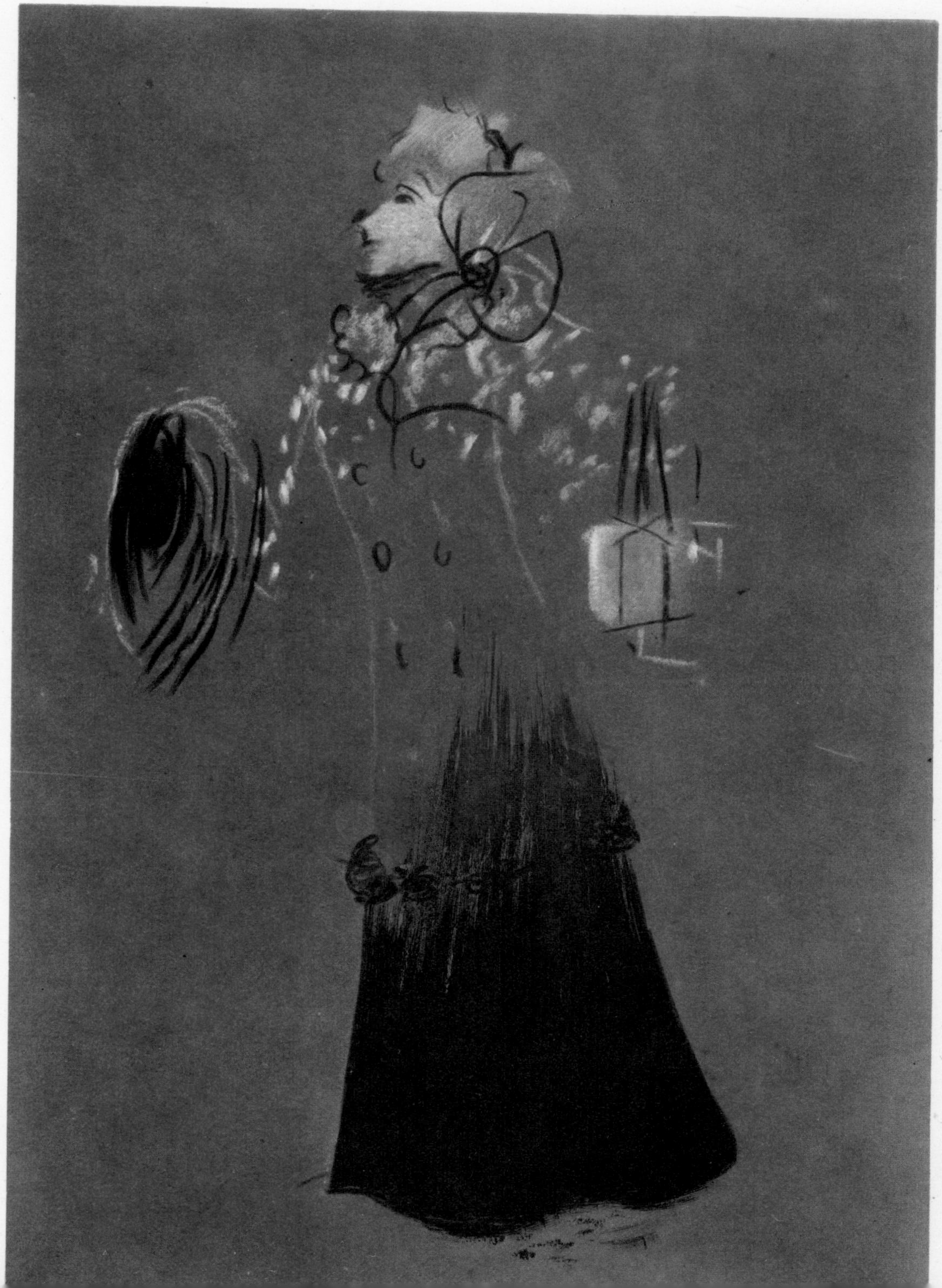

285

286

287

288

Designs by Stanislav Kolíbal

163

289

Designs by Stanislav Kolíbal

ANTON PAVLOVITCH CHEKOV

Three Sisters

The eldest was called Olga, the middle one Masha and the youngest one Irina. Olga teaches in a lyceum and the people in the small town already consider her an old maid. Masha was eighteen years old when she married a college professor by the name of Kulygiṅ; she was then duly impressed by him, he was so sagacious and wise, but now she knows that he is an empty man. The youngest one, Irina, the "white bird", is their pet; she would like very much to do something useful, accepts a post as a telegraphist but the work is spiritless and dull, she changes her profession but it is no better.

In the first act, Irina celebrates her name-day. She says on this occasion: "We are three sisters and our life has never been beautiful. It has choked us like weeds . . . One has to work, work and work! And as we are doing nothing we are sad, joy is unknown to us and therefore we see everything so dark. Because we do not know how to work! We grew up in a family which hated work."

If only that sad lot could be changed by work — by any work! Irina is trying it but in vain. Life in a gubernatorial small town flows along like a lazy, muddy river and the plague of provincialism creeps steadily everywhere. Andrey, the only brother of those three sisters, has already succumbed to it. He wished to be a scholar, was the hope and pride of the family — but married a provincial hussy who developed into a bad-tempered, quarrelsome woman. Now Andrey has a post with the municipal administration, serving under the lover of his wife. Embittered by disappointment he is already on the other bank, among the superficial, empty people.

To tear themselves away from this *milieu*, to go away, very far, that is the desire of those three sisters. To Moscow! — the Moscow which is here the symbol of a better, more human world. But only a beautiful dream and cruel reality have remained. In this lies the dream of those three sisters.

290

166

291

292

167

293

294

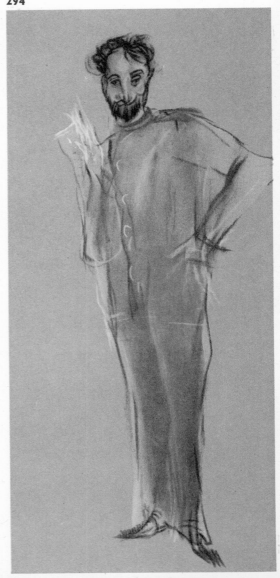

296

297

The Cunning Little Vixen

It began like this: a forester fell asleep in the wood and small forest animals of all kinds romped around him; a frog jumped on his nose, the forester, half-asleep, caught instead of the frog a small vixen. He brought her home and when the vixen bit a boy who teased her, he tied her to a kennel; our vixen, however, released herself from captivity, returned quickly to the woods and having driven the grumbling badger out of his lair, quickly appropriated a fine home.

In the fine warm summer night which followed the moon shone brilliantly and lured our vixen out for a short night walk. Something moved in the bushes and in a clearing appeared the he-fox Goldfleece, such a young and stout fellow that the Cunning Little Vixen could only sigh in admiration. They made each other's acquaintance and began to talk just like people, the courteous fox laid a fine rabbit at her feet, one thing led to another and before daybreak in the wood a woodpecker married them without much ado.

And then? Little foxes appeared and on a sunny day the whole family went out for a walk; the Cunning Little Vixen wanted to make fun of Harašta, the poultry dealer. She had her fun but the unfeeling Harašta shot her and the little foxes lost their mother.

There is another lovely day, such as was at the beginning of the story; the forester is again resting his tired body in the wood, only this time he is somehow thoughtful and sad, recollecting his youth and thinking of love — and again catches a small vixen while a frog is hopping around, only this time it is the grandchild of our old acquaintance. But for the fact that the forester

298

shows his age more, and but for the grandchildren feels everything would be the same, quite the same.

The fox Goldfleece, when he praised the beauty and cleverness of the Cunning Little Vixen, called her in his enthusiasm the ideal of the modern woman, declaring that even novels and operas would be written about her. He was not far from wrong. A novel was written about her by Rudolf Těsnohlídek, Leoš Janáček taught her to sing, thus paving her way to the world opera houses.

Many dramatic allegories in which animals act as people — and vice versa — have been written. Janáček's opera is not a simile of this kind — it is more of a lyrical comparison, in which man is at one with the *milieu* from which he has arisen — namely nature — and from which he removes himself further away in the technical age — to his own detriment. This work is merry and again sad, mischievous and again melancholy; it does not abound in deep truths and does not intend to force on the spectator the author's own definite conception of the world and man. It is a work for people to enjoy, the fruit of ripe wisdom of life. The secret of its charm is perhaps just in this.

299

300

301

302

303

173

304

305

306

Designs by František Tröster

176

THE ČAPEK BROTHERS

The Insect Play

A truly unflattering, deliberately distorted mirror was reflected by this pair of authors, the brothers Karel and Josef Čapek, on human society — so that bad human habits, vices and even crimes should be shown up as much as possible. Of *The Cunning Little Vixen* we have said that it is actually a lyrical comparison; here, however, it is indisputably a dramatic allegory, where the human species is subject to microscopic investigation. In triple conquest — erotic, commercial and military — the Čapeks follow man's life and ascertain that everywhere "Right is might"; how shady means, murder not excepting, are used by those insect people to achieve their desired goals.

It is no wonder that this melancholy comedy aroused stormy applause on the one hand and indignation on the other. Those for whom it was intended, who recognise themselves in the disguise of volatile butterflies, killer cuckoo-flies or fighting ants, who without a prick of conscience sacrifice innumerable lives for a piece of ground between two blades of grass, raised their voices. Both sides, however, concurred in that the picture was too gloomy, that human virtues were not depicted — in a word that it is too pessimistic. Both authors strongly protested against this accusation — first they tried to pacify the critics as well as the public by the second, "optimistic" variation of the finale which, alas, is even worse than the first, then explained their intention, and in the foreword to the fourth book edition they defended themselves against the accusation of pessimism. In it they also called attention to the importance which in their comedy had been given to the figure of the Vaga-bond, the only human, non-insect element in the whole play, and wrote truthfully: "Every spectator or reader could have seen himself in the wandering Vagabond; instead . . . he believed he saw himself or his society pictured in the vermin which here had been made the bearer of evil." That is not only a clever excuse, it is genuine truth.

311

177

312

313

314

315

316

317

318

319

Designs by Oldřich Smutný

320

JOHN STEINBECK

Of Mice and Men

Our notes started with Verdi's *Aida*. A musical drama peopled with kings, princesses, and commanders, a drama of fatal passions, where the destiny of a State was at stake. We conclude our notes with John Steinbeck's dramatized novel whose heroes are two friends — farm labourers. This play is not concerned with the problem of a State but with the dreams of simple people who intend to buy a small farm which they would manage themselves and breed rabbits.

Steinbeck writes about humble people whom some fifty years ago writers did not consider worthy of interest. His George and Lennie wander about the south of the United States from place to place, working a month here, or even less there, because the weak-minded Lennie usually does something wrong — without bad intent — they are in trouble and have to leave in a hurry.

They are just settling down in a new job when misfortune overtakes them again; the huge and violent Lennie, not conscious of his great strength, kills a man. He is in danger of being lynched. And now his friend renders him a service which Lennie will never appreciate: to save him from torture and subsequent death, the cause of which he would not be able to grasp, George unexpectedly shoots him himself.

Although Verdi's *Aida* is by far not the first masterpiece in world drama nor Steinbeck's play the last, incidentally, the path of development, leading from exalted characters to ordinary people, opens out between these two.

322   323   324

325

326